BLACK SEA WHITE NIGHT

BLACK SEA WHITE NIGHT
Memoir of A Boat People: **Mộng Thường**
Transalor: Tran Sealy
Layout: **Nguyễn Thành**
Cover: **Lê Hân & Nguyễn Thành**
ISBN: 978-1989705889
Nhân Ảnh Publisher 2020
Copyright @ 2020 by Mong Thuong

MỘNG THƯỜNG
Transalor: Tran Sealy

BLACK SEA WHITE NIGHT

Memoir of A Boat People

NHÂN ẢNH
2020

Since the day the South was conquered by the communists, so many things happened in the society as well as in every family. From the trick to lure the officers of the Republic of Vietnam into education camps, to the campaign against 'comprador-bourgeoisie', the currency revaluation, confiscation of private property, forced relocation of city dwellers to the new economic zones and compulsory labor in irrigation projects, all these drastic upheavals paled before the mass panic of people running here and there to find a way to escape the country. There was a popular saying that "If a lamp post could walk, it would also try to run away".So did everybody, including me, who were trapped for one reason or another

FIND THE WAY TO ESCAPE

My escape of Vietnam by sea after the fall of South Vietnam to the communists was just like that of other boat people. It was a harrowing, costly experience with high risk of imprisonment if caught and death by drowning if not saved by God's grace.

After days of clandestine search for a guide to escape. I did not know how many times my family was duped and cheated. We lost the equivalent of a few bars of gold as advance to phony middlemen who took the deposit and never came back. There was a time when I got tired, depressed and lost faith,resigned to let go, come what may.

But every day, to hear the news that the child of Mr. and Mrs. X or the husband of B. had escaped and reached this or that country, I panicked and felt that I was doomed to spend the rest of my life with this horde of heartless human beings. It broke my heart to see my husband sigh at the prospect of an uncertain future, when every morning he got on a rickety bicycle to go to work.

His white Lambretta scooter was now just a heap of junk. The ebbs and flows of time had washed away his life of decent comfort. This happened not only to him but to everybody. His mother repeatedly told him to sell it because keeping it in the house was an undeniable confession of the bourgeois background of the family. But he and I did not want to part from it, a souvenir of our time of love. I said to him we would bid farewell to it when we escaped from here. It was a daily reminder of our wish to get out of this land of injustice and servitude, only then that we and our compatriots in the South could see our future. So I put on the cap, got on the bicycle to meet my acquaintances, relatives and asked to join them if they were attempting to escape.

After night after night of burning incense and praying, asking the Almighty to find a decent ship owner to help us with the safe escape, God had finally answered my prayer. I finally found a lead through a relative who had his relatives safely escape but the fee was very expensive.

At that time, the semi-official fee of escape for the Chinese Vietnamese was from 9 to 10 gold bar (one bar is equivalent to one *lượng*[1]) for each person. My connection was not semi-official, but the owner still asked for 10 bars for one adult and 5 bars for children under 10. Advance payment was half of the fee; the rest would be paid up after the successful transfer from small boats to the big boat. A secret message would be given to the ship owner as proof and the remaining half of the fee in gold would be paid to the ship owner.

Our family consisted of my husband. Me and 3 children. The oldest child was 4 years old, the second 3 years old, and the youngest was under one year. In ad-

---
[1] One *lượng* = 37.50 gram gold bar

dition there were also two younger sisters, one younger brother and a nephew – a ten year old son of my eldest sister; altogether 9 persons of the family.

Carrying the bulky amount of gold hidden in our body to be paid as down payment to the wife of the boat owner during our overnight stay at the temporary shelter required extremely discreet and secured packaging. My mother had to make a few long 'elephant-gut' belly packs to carry the gold, which was then wound tightly around the waist of the grown-ups of the group.

Escape was the decision of my husband and me, which was strongly discouraged by our parents because of the high risk of extreme unforeseen danger of the high seas, starvation and sickness.

Fortunately, during this time, in the neighborhood I did not hear any bad news about people who had escaped. We heard hearsays of boat landing safely in Malaysia, rescued by foreign merchant ships, or picked up by Caritas ships[2], etc.

These rumors reinforced my confidence that the trip would be a success. My husband asked me to bring along his sunglasses for him to wear when getting on the big ship. So sunglasses were added to two sets of clothing, together with some foods personally cooked by my sisters consisting of crushed peanuts and steamed-sticky rice tightly pressed into truncated cone-shaped

---

[2] 'Mission Vietnam', a humanitarian initiative was carried out in 1979 by the Marina MilitareItaliana (the Italian Navy) ... "in 45 days of mission the ships and the embarked helicopters explored 75.000 square miles and took on board 902 displaced persons." The Boat people saved – including men, women, elders and children – were harbored in the Italian territory thanks to the support of volunteer groups and civil society organizations, like the Red Cross and the Italian Caritas. http://www.iitaly.org/magazine/focus/op-eds/article/way-we-were-humanitarian-missions-and-boat-people-yesterday-and-today

Mộng Thường | 9

lumps that could be kept unspoiled for a week. This preparation was learned from the experience of people who had helped relatives to escape or to go to political re-education camp.

DEPARTURE

I remembered very clearly that evening, mid-September 1978, the day of our departure. The ship owner said that after dinner, we would be picked up at the corner of PhuTho race course. We were told to follow the guide wearing a blue shirt who would approach us and said a secret password. The nine of us were split into small groups to go by cyclo to the home of one of the organizers. Early next morning we would go to the bus station to take the west-bound bus to Vinh Long and Rach Gia.

My husband went with our second son;the oldest son and youngest son went with me. Another separate group consisting of our two sisters, brother and nephew also took a separate bus down the rendezvous. From that moment we were not to see each other again.

That year there was a very big flood in Region 4. The road to Vinh Long was completely gridlocked.With flood water level over the wheels, many vehicles broke down along the road causing an impassable bottleneck. So my sons with me together with the guide and other passengers had to spend the night on the bus right on the road, surrounded by nothing but high sky canopy and immense expanse of water.

The bus was crowded and suffocating; mosquitoes swarming in the dark had to be brushed away by constant waving of the arms. My two children cried aloud, frantically jerking their heads.

Poor children! As soon as they opened their mouth to cry, the mosquitoes rushed in, causing them to choke and cough. My eldest son – being pampered from a young age and now exposed to suffocating heat– cried out loud until he lost his voice, demanding to go home with grandpa and grandma. Myself, I felt extremely tense and exhausted. Having been used to have someone to look after my children, now faced with two tired, hungry, crying children I panicked, not knowing what to do. A kind, old peasant woman asked:

- Why are they crying so miserably? Or is it a tummy ache?

- Madam. It's the heat and constant mosquito bites, they can't stand it anymore.

I answered, digging into my bag to look for the vial of Nhi Thien Duong oil to rub the children. It was a pitch dark night, not even a twinkle of starlight, one could not see one's own open palm; only the constant buzzing of insects and the noisy croaking of the frogs, and now the shrieking of children. Even grownups like me were scared, let alone the kids. Exhausted from crying, the children fell silent for a while only to squeal again because of mosquito bites. I had never been through a night as long as that night.

By the following morning, because of the bus breakdown and the rising water level, passengers were ferried part of the way by a small sampan. This was the first time I ever set foot in Region 4 so I did not know where I was, and only followed the guide. At noon the guide took me and my children to a roadside eating hut. But upset and anxious, I could not make myself taking any food.

I just sat, staring at the plate of rice, tears flowing down my cheeks. The guide reminded me again and again not to do so for fear of drawing the attention of the police. After lunch, we rested while waiting for the cycle rickshaw to carry us to Rach Gia. In the afternoon, I heard the guide gave instruction to the driver. We sat in the passenger seat in front and the guide sat behind us.

The area was also flooded, but the water level was not as high as in Vinh Long. The road was unsurfaced and we had a bone rattling rough ride. When the vehicle had just turned into a corner of the market, I saw my husband holding hand with our second child walking in front of us.

The skinny boy, probably deprived of the usual loving care at home, looked exhausted, hurrying on staggering steps with his father toward my arriving cycle rickshaw. By natural reaction, I was about to call out, but stopped right away, remembering the ship owner's instruction to absolutely not recognize each other as relatives once we were on the road. So I just discreetly glanced at them and caught the sight of my husband also recognizing his wife in the rickshaw cart.

Arriving at the docking area for commercial and private boats the guide told the driver to stop and we had to walk a long way to get to a house (which I knew later was the ship owner's house).

One hand holding my youngest son on my hip, the other leading the older child,on my back a bag containing foods, a few cold medicines as well as sleeping pills and some clothes for the three of us, I waded on the still flooded road,trousers rolled knee high, toward the boat.

In front of the boat stood a man about 40 years old, hale and healthy looking, with a strong composure and bright eyes under black eyebrows.His shaved head with bristling short hair gave me a creepy impression that this man might not be of a simple type.

The guide deftly stepped on a narrow wood plank-serving as a gangplank to the boat, making the boat rocking. I felt dizzy and scared and did not dare to step on the plank. Seeing that I kept groping around and not getting in, she ran back to pick up the two children and brought them on to the boat first. I trembled while crawling on the plank for fear of falling into the river. As soon as I got in the boat, the ship owner chided me:

- You are a city dweller but you do not take care to hide your identity, rolling up your pants so high with white legs sticking out,do you want to be caught?

Rattled by his warning, I meekly mumbled my excuse:

- I do not know, the water level is so high on the road.

No answer, but he threw at me a look not very sympathetic. I looked around at the boat, about eight meters in length, and three meters wide. This was a dwelling boat, where the family lived. Behind the compartment area was a little higher section with a mahogany bed- where there was a radio cassette with cassettes, plus the beddings, blankets and pillows of the owner. Deep inside, at the end of the boat was the kitchen with an oil stove, a charcoal stove, a cupboard for bowls and dishes; pots and pans were hung on a wooden stick. Dinner was being prepared there. Only half an hour later, my two sisters and nephew were put into this boat. Meeting each other, but we were all silent not daring to talk or ask each other, the face of each child was very tense. I wanted to ask my two sisters about their brother? Since separated at the corner of PhuTho race track I did not have any news about him, but no one knew.

ON A SMALL BOAT

Dinner over on the boat, it was getting dark. Suddenly the ship owner jumped into the river and swam somewhere for a while, then he came back and talked to the guide, and right away my two sisters and the nephew were transferred to another boat.

I had thought that if this boat was the only place to receive people from the city, why did they not bring my husband and my second son here? This afternoon I saw the two of them walking in this direction. But I did not dare to ask. Seeing that after dinner we were still on the boat, my older son asked me:

- Mama! Do we go home now? I want to sleep with Miss Linh.

I quietly coaxed him:

- We'll wait for Daddy and then go out by boat.

He squirmed and burst out crying:

- No, I want to go home. Mummy! I want to go home.

The owner of the ship, named Uncle Six, scowled at me and ordered:

- Give them the sleeping pills, then you three will go to another other boat.

I hastened to comply to his order, making my children take the sleeping pills, mix the medication with trembling hands. My youngest son, still on bottle feeding at the time, it was easy to give him sleeping pills, just by putting it in the bottle. But my older son was more difficult, at home making him take medicine was always a problem. Now it was even more difficult, he cried, refusing to take the medicine. Annoyed, the ship owner pointed at my son and said harshly:

- Give this brat a strong dose, to keep him quiet. In a few minutes, you will be transferred to a cargo boat, then early in the morning you will go to the landing area to get to the big boat. If he cried, he will be strangled by the helmsman. I warn you in advance so that you know what to do.

I was shocked, casting an incredulous, cold stare at the ship owner. Seeing my horrified expression, he repeated:

- I'm not kidding. Do you still want to go now? But if you want to continue, I won't guarantee the life of this boy!

With a tearful voice I pleaded:

- Uncle Six! I am determined to go, the gold has been delivered to you.

He interrupted:

- Don't worry about that. If you do not go the gold will be returned to you. I find it best that you take your son back to Saigon.

- But my husband and another child, why are they not here yet? I hurriedly asked.

- They are in another boat leaving at night. So do you want them to cancel the trip? I will contact to tell them to go back to Saigon with you.

Right away, the ship owner stood up getting ready to jump into the river to go to my husband. I sprung up and said in a pleading tone.

- Uncle Six! Do not call back my husband. Just let him go.

Then, clasping my hands, I pleaded with him:

- Please let us go with you. I already gave my two kids the medicine. They are sound asleep now.

BE TAKEN ABOUT

But despite my pleading and entreaties he only agreed not to go and tell my husband.But he ordered me to pick up my belongings and leave the boat immediately. He even refused my request to look for the sandals of my son that I carefully put at the bottom of the boat. Right away, he told the guide to take us to a house nearby to pass the night and get on the bus to go back to Saigon early next morning.Without sandals, the oldest son must go barefoot on the jagged stone, he cried all the way. Seeing his legs bloody and swollen, my heart ached but I could not help him because I was holding my youngest son on my hip and could not carry him. So we kept on walking and crying.

I knew from that very moment we would be on separate ways, not knowing whether we would meet again. Only yesterday we were together under the same roof, but today each of us was on a different journey into an uncertain future.

I blamed myself for what happened now. If I had known, I could have stopped and talked with my husband that afternoon so that, at least, he would feel reassured to know where we were going, or he might have decided stay together and cancelled the trip. Now that I had to remain behind, he would worry very much not seeing us on the boat. I kept asking myself:

"My love, was it a justified sacrifice on my part when asking the ship owner not to call you back, or was it something I would regret later?"

My poor youngest son! He kept on sleeping in my arms until the next morning when we were taken by the guide to take the first bus back to Saigon.

It was a big struggle to get on the bus. The coach was full, I pushed my older son inside, let him hold the bag. With one arm holding the youngest son on my hip and the other arm hooked on to the side of the bus, I stood on the last step at the back of the coach – where the bus driver assistant usually stood – I felt reassured to leave this place the sooner the better.

The bus ran very fast, bouncing up and down at every pothole, many times I thought I would lose my grip and fall off the bus. Each time the assistant driver pounded on the side of the bus to signal the driver to stop for someone to get off, I was excited at the anticipation of getting a seat inside to lessen the danger.

I needed to get out of here the sooner the better, to take the children home. Only then I could feel better, otherwise the children would die of sickness. Until then we had been away from home three days. Three days of hunger, lack of sleep and all kinds of anxiety, plus my older son kept on crying all day. I was afraid he would die. Fortunately, the flood water had subsided; hopefully we would be back in Saigon today and not sleep in the in the open air like the previous night. It was not until 9pm. that we could get to the station for west bound buses. Altogether we had been on the move for ten hours from Rach Gia to Saigon [a distance of about 240 km].

By the time we got home it was nearly 11 o'clock at night, all the lights had been off. I softly called out for my mother. Hearing my voice, she thought it was a dream. But at the sight of the three of us in tattered cloth, disheveled hair,the young boy sleeping on my shoulder, the big boy crying out to grandma, my whole family woke up.

After feeding the children and put them to bed, I related my story from the moment I left home until my return. My parents and brothers and sisters were happy that we to got home alive. They comforted me saying it was fate. Now we only waited for news from my husband and our sisters to see whether they succeeded.

My in-laws saw me bring the two children safely home and were happy that the older son had not been killed thanks to my refusal to follow the ship owner's order.

The following day my youngest boy fell sick. He got fever and diarrhea, staying all day in bed, haggard looking, vacant eyes widely opened. At that time I did not understand why he fell sick. But later it dawned on me that it was because of the night on the bus and the mosquito bites were so thick that his face was covered with red rashes as if he had had chicken pox.

Fortunately we had been sent back, otherwise he would be sick on the boat and we could not do anything while drifting in the open sea. I was horrified at the thought. In misfortune there might be a blessing. I had learned this lesson.

As mentioned earlier, under the agreement, half of the fee in gold was paid in advance. The rest would be paid by the people back home when a secret message was received from the person making the escape. At the time we left the house, my father told me that when getting on to the big boat, write home the following message:"Phú quý sinh Lễ nghĩa" [Prosperity breeds civility]

The ship's owner must come with the written message to be paid the remaining fee. Only two days later, the family received this piece of paper in my husband's handwriting, so my parents gave all the remaining fee, of course, minus the fee for myself and our two children.

From that day we anxiously awaited the news of the people who had gone. Members of our two families kept listening to VOA transmission to hear about the rescue at sea, and about the weather to find out if there were any shipwrecks. Those were the days full of stress and anxiety. My mother was so worried that her blood pressure became very high, and she coughed blood. My daddy was more stoic he kept the anxiety to himself. But the desktop radio was always on his side. Then after dinner, my father and my husband's father visited each other to exchange information they had heard.

It was lucky, the day after my return, people at my

husband's work place came to ask if he was sick because he had been absent for a week without applying for sick leave.

Pretending that I was very upset myself, I burst out crying saying that myself I did not know where he was and that I had heard rumor that he had an affair with a woman. Sometimes he did not come home after work. I could not stand it anymore, we had a very heated argument and he left home ever since. My theatrical acting was so good that everybody was deeply moved.

My performance was so perfect because at that time I was really worried about my husband's journey, about my mother in the hospital and my youngest child's illness. All these events made me cry my heart out. In fact, this tearful emotional outburst really helped relieve my internal tension and I felt better.For more than one week, my mind had been wandering in the nine clouds and I had lost all sense of reality.

FAILURE

One morning while sitting at the shop, I saw Mrs. Sau, wife of the ship owner,coming. I turned pale, sensing something not good.Mrs.Sau said the big boat had been captured by the coast guard after two days. Why, she didn't know. She only know that everybody on the boat had been captured and detained in the jail at Rach Gia.

This was a terrible shock for both families. Mrs. Sau reassured us that her husband would try to do everything to get everybody out of jail as soon as possible, but each adult - children were exempted – would have to contribute another gold bar to bribe the prison cadres. Upon hearing this suggestion, we all had some doubt, not knowing whether they were captured or cheated. Anyway, "fish on the chopping board" the danger was clear and real,we must find a way to get our loved ones out of prison as soon as possible.

My family had 6 people in jail including 2 children, we had to come up with another 4 gold bars. Just as Mrs. Sau promised, about a week or so later in the evening when I was about to go to bed at my parents' home –we spent time both at my home and my in-laws' because the children were sick and needed help from both families – I heard a knocking on the side door and a soft voice calling the name of my little sister's name. Recognizing it was my husband's voice, I excitedly called out and the whole family rushed downstairs. When the door opened, I saw my husband holding our second child sleeping in his arms, next to him were two younger sisters and the nephew, but the younger brother was absent.

After getting the food for the "ex-prisoners", the whole family gathered around my husband to hear about the journey and how he got caught. Mother was impatient because her youngest son was absent. So right away my husband had to say that my brother was not detained with the rest– people with children were housed in the collective camp – but was kept in the area for political prisoners, which was relatively less crowded.

In the collective area the dwellings were crowded;the detainees had to work every day, sometimes digging grave for executed prisoners. (This detail we learned later from my brother after his release. He himself had been ordered to do this job). And his nephew, 10 years old, but scrawny and looking like an eight years old boy, was kept in the area for women and children. So he was in the same section with his two aunts. Only the younger brother was detained separately in the youth section,no one had seen him or heard about him.

ARRESTED

That night, of course, I stayed up to hear him recount what happened after we saw each other in Rach-Gia Market. In a steady voice, he said ....

My husband's account

Immediately after seeing the three of us on a buggy, Tu and I were taken to a boat. They told me to give Tu sleeping pills and they pushed both of us to the lowest compartment of the boat. I saw many people already down there. They lay quietly. It was dark so I could not see if our sisters and brother were in the same boat. I said to Tu: "You would fall asleep soon and do not talk to me anymore. Try to lie down here for a moment, and then you would feel better when we leave this place". Tu quietly nodded, showing his understanding.

About a moment later, I saw them piling up sugar canes over the opening to the bottom of the boat cellar where we were. When the sugar canes were stacked high, I felt suffocated because the sugarcanes had cut off the fresh air. I felt sorry for Tu. Lying next to him, I heard his difficult breathing, and was afraid he would not be able to stay in the cellar for long. It was stifling hot and dark, and with the sugar canes stacked close to our face, even an adult could not stand it let alone a child. Lying there for a long time, I did not know how many hours since the moment we were pushed down the cellar after dinner.

They had to pretend that the boat was carrying sugar canes to get pass the police checkpoint on the way to meet the big boat. I guessed that the boat began about midnight. After nearly two hours, it met the big boat. On the way people were absolutely quiet, one could only hear the putt putt of the motor and the water rushing by the bow of the boat. I heard the voice of the boat driver responding to the police checkpoint he was passing through. Every now and then he pretended singing a very sentimental song to distract the attention of the police.

In the boat compartment, everyone was as quiet as a mouse. Occasionally I reached out to touch Tu's face to see if he was still asleep or awake. The poor boy was sweating profusely. I felt sorry for him and silently prayed that if we got through this trip safe and sound I would adopt a vegetarian diet to show my gratitude for the protection of God and Buddha. I also did not know whether your small boat had left to meet the big boat and I looked forward to meeting each other on the big boat.

When the boat had gone past the police checkpoint without being questioned I felt relieved, and so was everyone in the boat. Upon reaching the estuary to meet the big boat, I only saw our sisters and brother thrown into the bottom of the big boat. Tu – being a small child– and myself – having to write the secret message for them to collect the remaining gold – were allowed to sit on the deck, which was more like a small loft. However, it was quite a relief sitting there to breathe the sea breeze and watch the heaving high waves.

After arranging for Tu to sit still on the floor of the big boat, I went here and there and asked some people whether they were on the small boat with you, but no one knew. Altogether there were 4 small boats to carry people. By that time, I knew that you three were not on this big boat. I did not understand why. I kept on asking myself but could not find an answer. I felt very tense because after people had got on the big boat, the driver started the boat, and I still did not know what happened to the three of you.

Contrary to my imagination before leaving, I thought big boat ought to be bigger than the boats I had seen. Alas, it turned out the boat was only slightly bigger than the boat carrying sugar canes in the morning. But we had reached the point of no return.

The boat had moved almost one day, when I heard people at the bottom of the board shouting in panic that too much water was coming in the boat and there was a danger that the boat might sink. In fact, from the deck one could see the waves higher than the boat, strong wind rocked the boat. Terrifying white crested waves kept rushing against the boat. People yelled and prayed.

I had to firmly hold Tu's hand for fear that he might be swept into the sea. Since the boat had been going on one day, I guessed we had covered a good distance, as I saw the dolphins swimming close to the ship. Poor Tu was hungry and cold but he did not cry or complain or at all, since late yesterday until now we had nothing in the stomach, not even a sip of drinking water.

[*Listening to my husband, I broke into tears. Looking at my son sleeping soundly in my arms, I said;*

- *Poor child! He was really brave, darling.*

- *Yes. It was really pitiable. My husband said.*]

Then he continued.

Until evening the boatman said the boat could no longer run, so he moored the boat at an island with beautiful scenery and clear sea water (later I learned it wascalled Tho Chu island). The kindhearted villagers provided us with sweet potatoes and cassava. They knew immediately that this boat was carrying refugees, and told us that by tomorrow morning, the police would come to arrest us. Everyone was dumbfounded and scared. But where to run now?

Hearing that people on the boat secretly threw all the gold into the sea to get rid of the evidence.Looking down at the water, I saw the sparkling gold bars falling into the water. Some were hidden by the rocks at the bottom. Just like what the islanders said. At early dawn, the police arrived and arrested everybody. Myself, I did not have gold, but only dollar notes rolls disguised as cigarettes in the cigarette pack you gave me. Seeing people throwing gold away to get rid of the evidence, I did the same by burying the cigarettes pack in the sand becausethe pack would float on the water.

[I gasped:

- What a waste! That dollar pack was worth a few gold bars

- I know, but then I had no choice. I thought I'd rather throw it away than let it fall into the hand of the police so that they could keep it to themselves and used it as evidence to accuse us.]

I nodded slightly in agreement with him. But in my heart I still felt sorry for the loss.

My husband continued...

GOING TO JAIL

The Border Police came in the morning. They herded everyone onto a fishing boat and returned to Rach Gia prison. They listed the names and sorted us out as follows: women and children in one place, single men and male youth in a confined area. However, men with children were detained in a relatively larger area. Knowing that, I told Tu to tell them that he was with daddy only and not with uncle and aunt. I emphasized: "You must said so, otherwise they would separate you from Dad and we might not see each other again. "Tu seemed understand the importance of what I told him; he nodded understanding and did not ask any further. I felt reassured.

After being assigned to the detention area, Tu and I were taken into a section for people who had been detained for a long time, so the ward was not as crowded as other wards– I later knew. Most of these prisoners were jailed for political reasons. On the first day, I was fortunate to meet a political prisoner, a few years older than me. When he saw me come in with Tu on my arm, he asked quietly:

- Are you arrested on the cross-border crime?

I nodded. He said:

- I'm in for political crime. You have a small child; tonight I will let you use my place with mosquito net. Sleeping without net he will be killed by mosquitoes.

Deeply moved by his kind offer, I just asked for Tu to be with him, myself I could sleep without the net. But Mr. HL (political prisoner) insisted. I did not expect that in misfortune we could meet such a benefactor. In the following days, whenever he worked in the kitchen Mr. HL would smuggled out a lump of burnt rice for Tu. After a few days, due to the poor hygiene in the prison ward, Tu's mosquito bites turned infected. I felt terrible to see him scratching himself until the pusand blood oozed out; but there was no medicine. So every morning HL brought Tu to the well nearby to bathe him. But it only got worse. The water discharged from the bathroom also ran into the well.

I anxiously hoped every single day to contact the family so that they could try to get me out. But there was no way to do so. I did not know whether the ship owner knew about our detention. I could not even contact our sisters and brother because they were kept in a different section.

The first day of questioning the police asked whether we tried to escape. I made up a story that my wife died and the child was sick, so I took him to look for medicine. He asked me the name of the hamlet chief but I could not answer. Mrs. Sau did give me a travel permit with the name of the hamlet chief but I carelessly put it in my pocket without reading it, not anticipating that we would be arrested.

A baby-faced cop shouted at me:

- Looking for traditional medicine in the countryside, how come you wore jeans?

Did you try to escape? If you are not sincere you'll stay in jail forever.

I still resolutely stuck to the same statement, come what may. I had lost everything. I didn't know what happened to you three. I and Tuwere in jail. The money was gone. What else could make me afraid of them? I forgot to mention that after questioning, they searched all over my body. Fortunately I had taken off the wedding ring and, not knowing where to safely hide it, I thrust it at the bottom of the jean pocket and prayed to God they would not find it. Thank God my prayer was answered; after returning to the detention ward, I still found it at the same place. That was really a miracle.

My husband asked me:

- When did the family know we are in jail?

- About a week after my return to Saigon. We heard from Mrs. Sau.

Leaning on the chair, he continued:

In prison we were cut off from the outside world. I wanted to let the family know but could not find any way. I asked around to see anyone was about to be released so that I could ask him to give the family a message to try to get me out. Also I did not want Tu to stay there for fear he would fall sick; the living conditions were terrible: lack of hygiene, nothing to eat, every day we were given each a bowl of sorghum plus a piece of half-cooked cassava. He got scabies all over his body. If our oldest son was in that state he would certainly die but Tu was very resilient. He could take it fairly well. He never cried. The ward was full of adults.Sometimes, out of boredom, some of the long-stay prisoners would encourage Tu and a boy two years older and him to have a wrestling match; the winner would get a bit of extra food. But Tu would do it, not because of food but because it made the room more lively. Everyone cheered, so they liked it.

I frowned in protest:

- Why didn't you stop it? They could be hurt.

- It's just fun. Anyway, they are children.

By the fourth week, one morning we were called to the office to have our bags back and told we were released. I was so happy; I embraced Tu telling him we were leaving. Coming to the front room we met our sisters and brother together with other people on the boat.We knew that it was the work of the ship owner. We were even given money for lunch and bus fare back to Saigon.

Before going to the bus station, I bought some foods and necessary items and returned to the detention center to have it given to HL. A fellow passenger on the boat advised me not to, out of a superstition that a person once released came back to the prison would run the risk of being in jail again. But I insisted on going back with the gift to show our gratitude to Mr. HL for his help during my imprisonment. If Tu had not been given Mr. HL's place to sleep under a net he would have suffered from mosquito bites very badly.

Tears came to my eyes at the thought that if that evening we had not been abruptly chased off the boat by Mr. Sau, my two youngest children would certainly get very sick in the harsh conditions of the prison. As it turned out, my bad luck had turned into a good luck. Life was so unpredictable and full of surprise.

Then I told him about the extra bars of gold we had paid to the ship owner to help bribing my husband and other family members out of jail. We had to pay dearly for it but the importance was to get my dear ones home.

After telling all about the hardships in prison, he told me more about what he had seen at sea.

He asked me:

- Do you remember I asked you to bring my sunglasses? I thought we would get on a big boat, with a deck and bunker beds. It turned out the boat was just a bit bigger than the one carrying sugar from Rach Gia and yet the ship owner loaded on it 126 persons.

When our big boat came near international waters – so I thought –huge waves continuously heaved the boat to the high crest and pushed it down to the deep trough. I thought if we were not caught, we certainly would have left our body on the high sea.

He said that it was a blessing that I and the two children had been sent back otherwise we would have ended in prison, suffering from hunger, misery, suffocation. If our oldest child had been in jail like his younger brother he would have died.

The day we left home we were nine people including adults and children. Now only my brother had not been released. We contacted Mrs. Sau to inquire about his condition, but she said he was with young able-bodied men, who had to go to work everyday so Mr. Sau had not been able to do anything for him yet. He had been in prison nearly two months, a few weeks longer than my husband. Poor boy! He was still at the age of going to school and enjoying life, living under the protection of the family. Now in prison, he must be very scared and miserable. He was only 14 years old, then. My mother was very concerned about him, she prayed for him every day; she even went to consult the fortune teller to know when he could be released.

One evening, after the dinner, Mom was about to close the shop, a young man with a headgear covered most of his face, stepped in quickly, pointing at a bag and said:

- Let me buy a bag.

My eldest sister picked up the bag and handed it to the customer, and, recognizing him, she howled:

- Mommy! Huyech is back..

'Huyech' was his pet name. He usually told jokes or did playful tricks to make us laugh. That day, released and coming back home, he knew the whole family would be happy, especially Mother, he being the youngest son. My whole family was ecstatic to see him home. So, the whole family was happily reunited.

HIDING

Our joy hardly over, when we had to face another worry. Having been told that my husband left home 'for a new mistress', his office asked me to advise him to go back to work. They even gave me a letter signed by the chief himself asking him to go back promising no disciplinary measures. But my husband's brother advised us not to believe what they said. They pretended to believe that my husband quit because of family quarrel but in their mind they assumed that my husband had escaped.

During this time both my extended families were on pins and needles. Youths rejected by their school due to long absence from school without legitimate reason were often drafted by the local committee to work as laborer in community irrigation projects. My mother had to pay some money to register as a noodle co-operative for the sisters to work. In addition they had to get piece work stringing strands of bamboo individually on wire to make bamboo curtains for state export. This work made their fingers and knuckles ached and swollen.

My spouse, though released from prison, was constantly hounded by employees of his agency, hiding in different places and sometimes even had to go to the home of his brother in the new economic zone in Long Khanh. Our own house was confiscated by the government.

Mrs. Sáu came and let us know there would be another attempt to make up for the unsuccessful trip l ast time. The gold paid to the ship owner would not be reimbursed but another trip would be organized instead.

My husband however insisted that he did not want to go on such a trip anymore. He didn't want to run the risk of being in prison again, and also it was very dangerous; life was just like a bell hanging on a flimsy thread. Previously he didn't know about the danger. But now, having gone through it, he would not let the family going that way any more.

He said that there was a B2 help hand (slang for secret police informant) on the boat. Everybody was arrested and thrown into prison, and it was luck that no one lost his life. If the flimsy boat had kept drifting for days in the stormy sea, we wouldn't know how many would survive? He looked at me while stroking on Tu's hair:

- .... Another thing, it was heartbreaking to see our innocent children dragged into such deadly circumstances.

Wiping my tears I meekly responded:

- But your condition now is already like riding on the tiger's back, no longer free to live with the family, and constantly on the move to avoid the police. How long can we live such a life?

Shaking his head, he forlornly looked at me. I caught a glimpse of despair in his eyes.

After a few days waiting with no reply from us, Mrs. Sau came to ask me about my husband's situation. I told her that he was not a military person and therefore not obliged to go to re-education camp but since his return from the failed escape attempt, he had lived a hard life going into hiding to avoid the police and the neighborhood authority. Mrs. Sau advised me to persuade him to leave, because he had no other choice. If he worried about the danger for the children, then this time he could go by himself. If he chose to stay but unable to live with you and the children then it would be the same. She also said that most of the passengers on the trip, agreed to try again. This time, learning from the experience of the previous trip, Mr. Sau would be more careful when hiring the assistant.

I talked to my husband and begged him to leave to end this life of a fugitive and to have a better future. My three children and I would stay. No matter how much I said, he remained unconvinced. He said:

- "One day in jail is like a thousand years out". Now

I understood and felt the meaning of that saying. Beside hunger and deprivation, there was the loss of self esteem and honor being subjected to the whims of an illiterate, uneducated young brat. I found it unbearable and unacceptable. I swear never in prison again at all cost.

Our "to go or not to go" plan ended in a deadlock. After several nights of thinking I suddenly remembered the letter from the manager of the agency where he worked, confirming there would not be any trouble when my husband returned to work. My husband told me to find a way to discreetly contact the secretary of the agency, who seemed to have sympathy for him and could tell him more accurately. I came to the agency, pretending to ask if my husband had come back to work and also casually met the secretary. She confided in me:

- Tell your husband not to go back to work at all cost. It is said the person wanting help him "may have a kind heart but no power". He cannot do anything else. Once your husband returns to the office, the police will arrest him right away. Everyone says your husband has tried to escape.

I cried, seeing that my husband had no choice but to leave. The secretary mistakenly thought I was suffering from being abandoned by my husband. I tried to justify for him and also to play out my acting:

- That's so unfair to my husband, although his leaving home has made me extremely miserable.

What the secretary said was the deciding factor for us; my husband had no other choice. Indeed every cloud had a silver lining. Seeing no way out, my husband had resigned to going alone.

I let Mrs. Sau know of his decision. It was the end of the year 1978. It was the last Christmas he spent with us. Mrs. Sau said on January 4, he would be picked up at the corner of Phu Tho race course.

My mother went to the fortune teller, a visually impaired man who told fortune by feeling the surface of three tossed coins. Exact date of birth of the person concerned must be given. The fortune teller said this trip would begin with difficulty but would have an auspicious outcome. My mother asked if he should go alone or with some other relatives, and he said the message of the oracle is to go by himself.

I didn't know if my decision to stay behind was right or wrong. I asked myself many times whether my sacrifice was right; I myself had sent him to his death? Or if his departure was successful, would he still think of our conjugal love, of the children growing up without their father? Would we meet again in the future? Life was full of uncertainty. I really had faith in him. But a lonely man living by himself, who knows what would happen?

My heart was like a ball of tangled silk thread. But eventually my love for him had prevailed. I told myself to accept the sacrifice. If he would go away forever, or had a change of the heart, that was my fate. I did not believe in fortune telling, but I believed in destiny, or karma in Buddhist teachings.

My life from birth to marriage had been drifting along with the ups and downs of the destiny of country; every happening had a cause. The fact that I was sent home by the ship owner hadhelped me avoid going to jail. If fate had not turned out that way I might have lost a child. Thinking like thatI felt at peace and found my decision was for the overarching benefit of others and was worth doing.

THE SECOND ATTEMPT

The day of my husband's departure, I remembered very clearly, was in the morning of January 4, 1979. We woke up when it was still dark. A slight aroma of burning incense waffled in the air and there was whisper downstairs. My in-laws had got up, offering incense on the altar to pray for his safe journey. After kowtowing at the altar, my husband drank tea with his father. The two of them sat quietly together, but it seemed they had said to each other thousands of things they wanted to talk about. It was only until 30 years later that my husband discovered that the ash and the unfinished part of the cigarette –he had smoked while drinking tea with his father–had been carefully packed and preserved by his father as a souvenir of the moment sitting next to his youngest son before he left on a fateful journey that boded more ill than well.

When my husband got up to take the bike to the gate, his father grabbed his hand and pleaded:

- Let me go with you a short distance.

My husband bowed down to hide his tears, saying in a moving tone:

- I think it may not be convenient. Just let me go as I usually go to work, to avoid the eyes and ears of the police.

The gate behind my husband and me had not been closed; our father still held on to it, tilting his head, following the two of us with his eyes.

We rode the bike together to the rendez-vous. Sitting behind him on the baggage rack, holding the bag that would be with him on his journey, I tried to hold back the tears brimming in eyes, not daring to cry, for fear it would make him sadder. Only when I rode back by myself that I let my tears flow freely. I knew from that moment we might no longer see each other again. Even if his trip was a success, how could we find each other again in this immense world?

I did not expect my life to be so lonely again. Looking back from the day we embarked on the idea of escaping, everything had happened so fast that I did not know where I was. Was this a dream? I kept asking myself. Suddenly I felt empathy for women having their husband in re-education camp. We only commiserate with each other when we are in the same boat. Oh! The tragic destiny of a nation had a terrible impact on its people, from newly born babies to adults; everybody endured the pain of loss and separation.

Coming home to see the closet full of pictures of him, the bed with pillows blankets still wafting with his scent, I could not stand it. I was like a lost soul, only wanting to be alone with my loving thought about him.

But I could not do so, when my children still needed me. Fortunately, we received help from both sides of the family. My mother asked me to live at her place where I could get help from my sisters to care for the children. But I pleaded with her to let me stay with my husband's family so that I could continue to see his pictures.

After a lot of persuasion, my mother consented, but she wanted me to bring the two children to stay with her during the day – leaving my oldest son at the care of my husband's mother – and returned to our paternal home in the evening. I had to shuttle back and forth between the two homes to avoid being drafted as laborer for irrigation projects. Moreover, the local police would not notice my absence from any home in case I might one day plan my own escape.

The days waiting for news from my husband, I was like a person sitting on fire. My dad and father-in-law spent every night hugging the radio in bed to listen to VOA news. Sometimes I ran to the house of Mrs. Tu – a close friend of Mrs. Sau and also having relatives on the same rip with my husband – to ask for news. But nothing was heard. Streets were becoming more lively with the approach of the Lunar New Year.

Every morning after bringing the two children to my mother's house, I sat in the store looking forward to hear from Mrs. Sau. Day after day went by, my heart sank deeper and deeper into anxiety and somber premonitions. Indeed, nothing could be more tormenting than those feelings.

Then one day, Mrs. Sau finally came with the news that the trip could have gone well because no one from the boat crew had been reported arrested. That meant the boat had escaped the police but would it have escaped death in the open sea? I had heard from my husband about the huge waves in his first attempt. Every night before going to bed, I stood on the balcony with burning incense to beg for the blessings of the Almighty and Buddha for my husband's safe and sound passage.

One day while putting my child to a midday nap, the mailman called out my name for the mail. I saw a thin envelope with apparently nothing inside. I hastened to open the envelope and saw a telegraphic message

- "Met uncleThai, do not bring children to swim."

Breathless, I woke up my parents from their midday nap and ran as if my feet were on wings to my husband's parents for the good news. An oppressive burden was suddenly lifted from our heart. The telegram meant that he had reached Thailand, and it implied that he advised me not to take the children on the escape?

MAKING DECISION

When joy had come and worry about his safety had gone, my thought turned to the separation between him and the four of us. From now we were in different worlds,how could we meet each other again?

I had a friend whose husband had been in reeducation camp nearly five years. Feeling sorry for her, occasionally, on my way with our children to my mother's,I would drop in to comfort her and to share with her the lonely hardship of raising the children and sending foods to her husband in the camp.

Now my husband had gone and might never see us again. Comparing my situation with hers, I suddenly felt more sorry for myself. Her husband was in prison, but at least she could still visit him. As for me, would I ever see my husband again? The thought made me feel my life no longer had any meaning, even though we still had the loving support of both our families. But deep down in my soul, I still found myself helpless and lost. At that time no one knew that there would be family reunion sponsorship program for refugees, it was definitely certain that my children and I would be stuck here forever. So from that day on I had determined to go.

I returned to Mrs. Tu's house to contact Mrs. Sau, but she was not always present in Saigon. So every few days I cycled there to find out if Mr. and Mrs. Sau were planning another trip. I confided my intentionwith my second sister. Initially she tried to dissuade me, seeing the children were still young, and the dangers at sea we ourselves had experienced. She advised me to give up this reckless attempt, and wait to see how my husband would settle in a third country. She advised me to stay and bring up the children with the support of the family. That was the view of an outsider.

Since married, we had not been apart for one day, except the time when my husband had to hide from the police after the first failed attempt. Now separated and maybe never seeing each other again, I knew both of us would suffer tremendously.

Among the passengers I met on the way from Saigon to Rach Gia in the first attempt, some were still staying because the trip my husband took had enough people, and they were not informed by Mrs. Sau. When they learned that my husband had succeeded, they asked Mrs. Sau to let them go on the nexttrip –the one I planned to take – so I would have more companions sharing my wish.

Learning that I still wanted to go, both my parents and my in-laws were very worried. It was lucky by that time the majority of children in my neighborhood succeeded in their attempts. The trips organized by the Chinese-Vietnamese, with the tacit approval of the government, sailed off in great number. Every few days there were news that this ship had escaped, that ship had reached safety.

At my mom's shop, every day people came, exchanging hearsays more than buying. I also heard stories of people interviewed by a United Nations High Commission, people on the list to be settled in a third country, others receiving news from their husband who had left on the day of the fall of Saigon. All kinds of information and rumors, most were good. Once it was said that a boat ran aground, everybody prayed in earnest, and suddenly tidal water rushed in from nowhere pushing the boat going its way.

These stories made my parents less worried if I ever decided to leave (so I thought). All that time I continued to keep contact with Mrs. Sau and kept on trying to convince my family. My in-laws, learning that I planned to bring the children along, strongly discouraged me.

I told them the positive stories I heard but still they were not convinced. Finally they came to ask my parents not to allow me to take the children if I decided to go, and left the children in the care of both families. But how could I go alone leaving the children behind? Maybe I would have to give in, grudgingly I stayed, and come what may.

While stuck in a mental dead end, not knowing how to decide, I received my husband's letter from the Songkhla Refugee Camp. So I was determined to leave no matter how dangerous. It also happened that Mrs. Sau said that Mr. Sau's younger brother would also be on this trip together with two nephews of Mrs. Tu. Seeing that this was a trip with members of Mr. Sau's family, and that I resolutely wanted to leave, my parents seemed reassured, and let my husband's brother and sister go as in the first trip. But this time there was only one sister withher brother and a nephew. When I spoke to my in-laws, I received the support of my mother-in-law, she told my father-in-law:

- Well, let's just let her take her children along. Her husband would be very upset to see her without the children.

- But his telegram said not to bring along the children, do you remember?

Then turning to me he stiffened:

- Do you know that you are taking your children to death? Poor kids, they are too young to understand.

I covered my face and cried, not knowing what to say to justify my reasoning. The only justification was the future of my children;they would be deprived of their rights of freedom and democracy as happened to all people in the South. My father-in-law, fearing forthe life of his grandchildren, refused to let them go. Life is precious. He would rather resigned to the fact that they would live in misery and hunger than putting them in a situation of possible death.

That year our two families had spent a not very happy New Year despite the good news from my husband. A somber mood hang over the family at the prospect of the children leaving on the trip with me. Usually on the days before the New Year, my mother would make rice cake. But that year, she could not have the heart to so. Whenever I was with her, she often reminded me:

- I let my children go with you, because I believe that you are wise enough to guide them. When you get there, take care of them on our behalf. Remember to love each other when living in a strange land.

I reassured her:

- Do not worry. When you trust in me like that, I will wholeheartedly remember your words.

To let her understand what I had in my mind, I said:

- Who know, maybe they will have to help me to care for the children. You know, from the day I got married and have children, you and they have always helped me take care of the children. Now, away from the family I am afraid I may notbe able to do it by myself. How can we not love each other? *Each is dependent on the other for mutual survival.....*

Mother seemed to be relieved. Later I realized that it was the last time she felt happy to see we all had pledged to do what she said. Also, mother and I did not know that it was the last time the two of us had been so close together.

Shortly after, it was time to leave. This time we did not have to bring the gold to pay the ship owner. The payment of my brother, sister and nephew was still with him. Only payment for myself and three children had not been paid. Now that we had known each other, it was agreed that the payment would be made to Mrs. Sau when my parents received the secret message –Homage to the Ancestors upon Graduation "Vinh Quy Bai To", drafted by my father - that we had got onto the big boat.

CHOICE

Usually things do not happen the way you plan. "Man Proposes, God Disposes" It's true in my case. Before the departure my eldest son fell sick.He had high temperature and felt drowsy all day. The doctor prescribed fever relief medication, but after a few hours his temperature rose again, it got worse in the afternoon.I had to leave next day in the afternoon, his fever had not subsided but I had to go. So my father-in-law insisted on not letting him go

Watching him in a state of deep sleepiness I knew that I couldn't take him with me. If I contradicted my family's opinion, I was afraid his sickness would worsen on the way and his life would be in danger. So, fighting to hold back tears, I had no other choice but to be on my way. With the youngest on my arm and holding the other in my hand, as I usually did in the morning when going to my mother's house. But this time, with an aching heart and weeping profusely, I felt very sorry for them because I knew difficulties and dangers were awaiting us.

I had to stop by Grandma's house to pick up my two younger siblings and nephew. Seeing that my eldest son could not go, my parents and siblings comforted me saying that according to the horoscope he would not be able to be with his parents until when he was 12 years old, otherwise he would be very sick often and might even lose his life.

Honestly, I didn't believe in fortune telling, but for horoscope, with the exact time and date of birth, the destiny predicted for each person would be like an analysis by a computer. No wonder that since his birth, though we had hired a domestic to help with his care, in reality my son had been taken care of by one of my husband's sisters. And now, when we had to run away, circumstances - unexpected but apparently predetermined - had made him separated from his parents

I had no other choice but to keep going as planned. That night all of us slept at Mrs.Tu's house, and left for Rach Gia early next morning. By this time the flood in the west region had ended so it was only in the afternoon that we reached the home of one of Mrs. Sau's relatives. I learned that the host's son had also been on the same trip with my husband and was now in Songkhla refugee camp.

I slept at Phat's house one night, early next morning when I woke up to prepare milk for my youngest child, I carefully checked the bottom of the vacuum flask where was hidden the gold my mother had given me for living expenses at the refugee camp. My mother had taken care to have it made into separate rings that could be sold separately for cash. Before leaving Phat's house, I lit incense on the altar to pray for a safe and sound journey.

OUT FOR SAILING

It was still pitch dark when Mrs. Sau led our group to a small boat to go to the open sea to meet the big boat. Fortunately this time the big boat was receiving people from other small boats. As my husband told me about the first trip, the big boat was actually only bigger than the small boat that took me from the shore to the sea.

Because I had a young child–the youngest boy under one year old – I was allowed to stay on the deck with family members of Mr. Sau's younger brother. My two younger siblings and nephew, along with my second son, were told to stay at the lower compartment with others. Just as my husband remarked, my second son was really brave. When he had to leave me to go with his aunt and uncle down to the bottom of the boat, he silently followed them, even though I had pleaded with other passengers – apparently more wealthy – to let him stay with us, but they refused. At dawn, the ship started running.

The boat ran smoothly that day, there were no big

waves, white crested waves sparkled in the moonlight, the sea at night looked so beautiful and dreamy. Every now and then I saw some dolphins hovering. I remembered my husband telling me that on the first trip he also met dolphins, but they did not swim with the boat but against it, so the trip ended up being caught. But this time, the dolphins swam along the boat; probably we would not encounter any trouble, so I thought.

The day I got on the big boat was still within the week of the full moon, if I remembered correctly it was about the full moon of 1979; big moon showed up in the dark sky with thousands of stars twinkling around. This was the first time in my life I had seen the sea at night. In addition to the sound of the boat running, and the water splashing against the speeding boat, I noticed the well-to-do people, i.e. the family members of the ship owner, getting ready to have dinner together.

They went by the entire family, so husbands moved briskly back and forth between the bow and the stern of the boat bringing food or water to their wives and children. I guessed they had also lived on the boat for many years.The way they moved from one end of the boat to the other on the gunnel rail looked very agile. But they did not share foods with anyone. Being family members of the shipowner, they brought along plenty of foods and water. Although I had some foods with me in my bag, I didn't feel like eating. I only felt a dry throat and wanted to drink. Fortunately, the day we left Phat's house, I filled the vacuum flask with gruel of brown rice flour mixed with milk powder for the youngest boy. Whenever he cried, I would pour the mixture into the feeding bottle for him to grab and drink.

Sitting on the haunches, hugging the boy for ten hours, my legs were completely numb. The woman next to me said that on the boat there was no place for urination, if anyone needed to go, they simply climbed to the side of the boat and did it openly. But the boat was moving and was so unsteady, how I could do this, so I just sat there stuck in the cabin.

Exhausted, I dozed off I didn't know how long. Opening my eyes again, I saw a glowing dawn in the distant horizon. Second day at sea. I heard people saying that the boat had entered international waters. Now there was no fear of being caught by the police and we only wished to be rescued by foreign ships. Right at that moment we saw a blurred silhouette of a ship the size of a hand in the distance. So the boat started heading that way to get closer. It took a few hours to see this ship clearly. It turned out that it was not a foreign merchant ship but an ordinary fishing boat, but we did not know from which country. Seeing that it was not a merchant ship, we did not approach and continued our course.

In the afternoon, suddenly the clouds came swirling and it rained heavily. Big waves heaved the boat up and down, swaying and tossing it from side to side. Everyone on board panicked, their clothes soaked with rain and seawater. With one hand hugging my son, and the other holding on to the bars of the hull, I kept praying. I remembered my mother and older sister told me to recite the name of Guan Yin for her protection.

The assistant on the boat shouted loudly to everyone on board to try keeping the boat steady,and to take turn to bail out the water. Everyone was vomiting.From the upper deck, I saw people sitting, their hair-disheveled, head resting on bended knees like prisoners on death rows, their body limp like wilted leaves.

Luckily I did not vomit; maybe because there was

nothing in the stomach, not even a drop of water. I did not throw up like the people next to me because they had had a full stomach not so long ago. My son also threw up and cried in fear. While comforting him, I thought of my second son who had been dumped into the lower compartment, not knowing how he was doing. My face grimaced, my throat dry, I hadn't had a drop of water in my throat since yesterday morning. When it was raining I didn't have the opportunity to catch a few rain drops because I was busy taking care of my son. The women next to me were provided with food and water by their husbands.

    I suddenly felt sorry for myself and guilty to my children for having dragged them into danger. If only our family had been on the same trip, surely my husband would have tried to find food for his wife and children.

CONFRONT THE PIRATES

After the heavy rain, the sky was clear again, but the moonlight shining into the sea gradually faded away; the sea looked darker than last night. Looking at the black sea like that, I suddenly got scared, and maybe because I was soaking wet, this fear made me feel feverish. Perhaps I really had a fever because in my half-awake state I saw the image of Guan Yin wearing a white dress, holding a pitcher of nectar surfing on the waves in front of the bow, looking at the boat.

Suddenly there was a loud cry:

- Songkhla!!! Songkhla!!!

Startled out of my vision I realized that the boat assistant cupping his hand around his mouth to ask an approaching fishing boat the direction to go to Songkhla. Following the direction of the fisherman, our ship headed in that direction. Around noon, there was another fishing boat, bigger than the one we passed. On the ship, there were muscular men stripped half naked, wearing loincloths, with heads shaved, some wrapped in towels, their faces painted with stripes of different colors. Without a word, we all looked at them with apprehension. I heard a few people in the boat yelling:

- Beware of pirates.

- Don't get near his ship.

- Come on, let's turn away!!

Hearing those words, the boat driver hurriedly moved away, and continued his direction. Seeing our boat was not heading in their direction, this ship started chasing us. Everyone on the boat knew that we had met the pirate ship.

They harassed our boat for a while, and then two guys jumped down on our boats and the guy on their ship threw down a rope about the size of our wrists to tie our boat to their ship. Getting near, we saw that their ship was several times taller than our boats, so much so that from the boat their ship looked like two-storey building.

After tying the boat, they dropped a rope ladder and signaled to people in the boat to climb the rope ladder to their ship. The assistant boatman told them we wanted to go to Songkhla. Hearing the word Songkhla they nodded, and signaled everyone to climb up. But by a sixth sense, many people in the boat did not believe and sought to evade them. They were afraid to see a small boat floating so close to a 2 or 3-storey ship like that in the immense sea. Climbing the rope ladder while the boat was tossed around by the waves created by the engine of the ship was extremely dangerous.

When most of us refused to go up, they angrily shouted and beat those who disobeyed; women cried in fear. Knowing that there was nowhere to run, everyone gingerly climbed up the rope ladder. Having had to sit on the haunches a long time, with little sleep and food and in constant fear, no one had enough strength to stand up on his own. People barely stood up before falling down again and again. Watching them tremble on the rope ladder, I was so nervous and scared, just one misstep and one would fall into the sea.

When it was my turn, I was so scared I trembled like a leaf, clutching my youngest son tightly. I couldn't stand up; I fell on my knees begging the pirate not to make me climb that ladder. But he snatched the boy from my arms and shouted in their language to another one on the ship. When this guy responded, he tossed my son up like a brick –the way builders in Vietnam throwing bricks from the ground up for people on the upper level to catch.

I was shocked and speechless. In a fleeting moment, I could see the horrified expression in my child's big eyes. Fortunately, I did not utter a cry, because if I did, my son would wriggle in protest and the pirate standing above might miss him. When that guy had left my son lying in their cabin, I frantically hurried up the rope ladder for fear that my baby would crawl around and fall into the sea. It was total confusion andchaos. People screaming, shouting, looking for relatives, the sound of enginer rumbling; no one paid attention to anyone. Everyone for himself.

While waiting anxiously for my turn to get on the ladder, I saw my two young siblings crawling out from the boat's hatch to the cabin. My sister had just reached the door of the cellar, reaching out to pull her brother, I rushed over asking with a tearful voice:

- Duyen, Huy! Where is Tu?

They were bewildered not knowing what was going on, I hurriedly let them know we were meeting with the pirates and they were yelling and pushing people onto their ship. As soon as I said this, I saw a man pushing my second son out of the hatch. I hurriedly ran to catch my son, because he could no longer stand up. Duyen burst into tears:

- Poor Tu and Nguyen (my nephew). Being children they were forced to sit at the lowest level, suffering from suffocation, being vomited on by people at the upper level.

Duyen added:

- Tu and Nguyen have a cold because the lower level was flooded with water. Do you know they fainted?

Only then did Tu tearfully cried and hugged me, perhaps because he saw the fierce looking pirates shouting on the boat.

Duyen pointed at the man who pushed Tu up from the lower compartment.

- Fortunately, this gentleman helped me, otherwise I could not climb up here, because I've been sitting on my haunches so long that I couldn't stand up.

Then, as she suddenly remembered, Duyen hurriedly asked.

- Where is Be?

I pointed to the pirate ship:

- I have to climb up there right now, because Be is up there already.

I was about to walk away, but stopped short:

- But how could Tu climb that sky-high ladder?

I didn't dare to tell them how they threw the baby up, because I just wanted to get all of us up there as soon as possible to take care of my young boy. But I definitely wouldn't let the pirates toss up Tu like they did with the baby. While I was wondering what to do, the man who helped Tu climb up through the hatch told me:

- Don't worry; let me carry him on my back up the ladder.

I turned to Tu and said:

- Hold on to his neck tightly, so that he can safely climb the rope ladder up to the big ship. Understand?

Tu nodded, pursing his lips. So this kind-hearted

man carried Tu on his back, the rest of us followed him. I held Tu with one hand, and gripped the ladder with the other. When reaching the deck, I saw my baby son sitting on the deck crying his heart out. I knew he was terrified not seeing his loved ones around. Oh God, everything happened so fast, how I could cope with the situation without the blessings of God and Buddha and the kindness of my companions.

When all the people in the boat had been brought to the pirate ship, they gave everyone drinking water and food. They even gave candy to children. My 10-year-old nephew, intrigued with the steering wheel, was taken by the helmsman into the cabin to touch it. I screamed and told him to stay away, not knowing what might happen. Some people at first thought they were pirates, and was wary of them. But seeing such treatment, people were less worried and hoped to be taken to Songkhla.

"WHAT A MISTAKE!"

Each person pursued his or her own thoughts, everyone held on to the hope that they would get where they wanted to. Sitting and hugging my son on the pirate ship, I suddenly remembered the gold rings my mother had hidden at the bottom of the flask. If the pirates took us directly to Songkhla or to other refugee camps, the gold would be lost; where would we get money to live in the coming days. At that thought, I left the two children to the care of my siblings, walked to the stern of the ship to see what happened to our boat. I wondered if I could jump down to the boat to get my bag. When climbing on to the pirate ship, worrying about the lives of my children, I had no time think about the bag.

The boat was bobbing up and down on the waves as it swayed from side to side. Fortunately, the pirates had tied our boat to their ship. Many times I pursed my lips to muster up courage to try to jump down, but each time an invisible force had kept me back. Without the gold, how could we buy food if we reached the shore?

But now I didn't have the courage to jump down. Every time I tried to jump, the small boat was pushed away by the waves. I stood for hours looking at the boat as if hypnotized but not yet able to get a chance. Finally, when I was about to decide to go for it, suddenly my father's advice flashed in my mind:

- Never let material possessions dominate your life, sometimes they may cause misfortune.

My father added:

- If we had stayed in the North because of attachment to our possessions, how could you have a [comfortable life] like today?

Suddenly my father's advice drawn from his own life experience struck my mind and I gave up the idea of jumping into the boat to get my bag.

Back to where I was, watching my two haggard children, I could not imagine myself daring to lead my children into a perilous sea journey sea like this. I didn't seem to be me anymore, but someone else in my clothing. Normally I was a faint hearted, afraid of both physicaland mental pain, even afraid of learning to swim. Yet I dared to decide to take my children on a journey like this without the help of my husband. Seeing my worried expression, the two younger brothers asked:

- What happened,sister?

I sat down, told them about my intention to jump down into the boat to get the bag. Duyen looked at me, dumbfounded:

- Are you crazy? Why so foolhardy. If we lost it then we lost it.

If you missed the boat and fell into the ocean, who would save you? Besides, I am not sure if they will let you keep it.

Whereupon I realized that I was really out of my mind. Even if I had succeeded, would they let me keep it?

Who know, when herding us on to the ship, the pirates probably had taken my bag.

They wanted us to get out of the way so that they could search and look for hidden gold, jewelry and dollars.

I forlornly shook my head as if to drive away my crazy thoughts and I hugged my youngest boy closely in my lap. Before I could do it, I heard shouting of the pirates coming from the bow, and saw two of them with an aluminum mug in their hand demanding the passengers to put dollars, gold, jewelry, watches into the mug. Those who resisted were shouted at and even beaten. Those who shook their heads – meaning 'no' –were roughly body searched.

I had to remove my gold wedding from my finger and gave it to them. Although this was a keepsake, I dared not argue for fear of being assaulted. I told myself their robbing could be considered as a fare we paid them to take us to Songkhla– loss of belongings is better than loss of life – so I didn't regret it. The reason why we wanted to go to Songkhla was because the previous boat had been there; that was the only place the boat driver knew, and we heard that the way to get there was closer than to Malaysia.

It was only now that I realized it was lucky I did not jump into the boat to get my bag. If I had, I would have to give it to them now. Worse still, I could have lost my life in the sea. I shivered at the thought, and did not regret anymore. One way or another if it was lost, it was lost.

Having robbed all money and belongings, the pirates guarded over us. In total, they had 6 men, 3 guys carried spears and axes to intimidate us. Even the adults were scared, let alone children, so we stayed away from them. The man carrying Tu up the rope ladder sat with us. He seemed to be alone; perhaps seeing we were a group of women and children, he stayed close in case we needed help. Tu was scared, he cried and called out:

- Daddy! Daddy! Where's dad ….

I had to coax Tu:

- Don't cry, we're about to see Dad.

When leaving home, I tried to convince them that we were going to Dad. But now Dad was nowhere in sight, only danger and misery.

- Where is his father? The man asked.

I briefly told him my husband had gone in a previous trip and had come toSongkhla camp.Now I took the two children. Later I learned that he was a former ARVN captain who had just come back from re-education camp

While talking, I saw a number of people retreating towards me, including people who were kneeling and bowing to the pirates. I turned pale knowing something was wrong, and saw three guys with spears and knives making signs to tell all the boat people to climb the rope ladder back to the boat. People were so scared, they huddled together, women and children were crying loudly. Someone asked people still hiding dollars or the gold ring to give them to the pirates;maybe they would let us stay. Among the people on the boat, only Mrs. Sau's relatives brought a lot of gold. Everyone knew that, because they were the owners of the ship and had organized many trips. They must bring a lot of gold. I heard a woman speaking in a Southern accent:

- Alright, now we give it to these guys, so when we get ashore you have to collect gold to reimburse me. OK?

- Just give it to them; we'll work it out later.... We're going to die soon, what's the point of keeping gold!

A few people chimed in with annoyance.

- Hey sister! Consider you do a blessing saving more than a hundred lives

I didn't know how much gold or money had been given, or not given, but the pirates still forced all of us down to our boat. They drove people from the stern and the bow of the ship, dragged them to the side of the ship and forced them to climb down. Everyone burst out crying because they were too scared. We both cried and prayed Guan Yin for her blessings. My limbs were trembling, I couldn't even walk, how to climb down the ladder, while it was already getting dark. Only a small misstep was enough to stumble into the deep sea.

When begging and pleading failed everyone had to climb down to the boat. Someone suggested that the boat man and the men climbed down first to check how flooded the boat was and bailed out the water, if necessary. Then the children and women would follow. Remember my experience that morning, I prayed that the pirates would not toss my son down like a brick. It's easier going down this time than to go up, but it was getting dark, if you didn't make it before nightfall, it would be tough. The sea was very dark at night. Although the pirate ship had electric lamps, the light could not shine down to the boat. If we had to come down then the sooner the better.

I asked the former captain and another young man to help carry my two children down. We told each other to keep looking up, feel for the ladder rung with the feet to step down and ask for help from people at the bottom to make sure not to fall into the sea.

My sister whispered to me:

- Keep Tu sitting on the upper deck with you, it was suffocating in the lower compartment. Poor child! He's

Mộng Thường | 73

also a kid, why did the ship owner make him sit down there.

I nodded in agreement, and disregarding the ship owner's protests, this time the three of us sat together. Tu still sobbed and called for Dad. He was brave, courageous and smart, observant and rarely bothering the adults. But now he kept crying, I knew he was not feeling well. My younger sister said that while in the lower compartment, he had caught a cold and fainted; he could not breathe, and did not have enough food and water. Poor children! Seeing them cry, I could not hold back my tears, trying to sooth and comfort them saying that we would see Dad again. Myself, due to some invisible force, I always thought that I would meet my husband after such dangers.

Now I realized that it was fortunate that my eldest son could not go.If he had, probably his life would be threatened. No wonder my husband's message had advised me not to take the children on the journey. Oh! If people had known about dangers like these, no one would dare to take to the sea. At the time of departure, the main concern was about the police, only on the open sea that they met face to face with real and deadly dangers.

Having got my two children, my siblings and nephew down to the boat, I felt relieved. I told my nephew to stay on the deck with me and my children. For some reason, there were still a few boat people on the pirate ship. Were they still trying to plead with the pirates to take them where they wanted to go? I found out that the boatman was begging the pirates to let go of a girl they wanted to keep. How terrible!!! No wonder I saw the girl's boyfriend still up there. Fortunately for this girl, the boatman, speaking Cambodian, had successfully persuaded the pirates to let the girl go. Later it became known that the couple had to come up with more dollars for the pirates.

After everyone had boarded the boat, the pirates took off the rope tying the boat to the ship.However problem was not over yet.Before leaving, they rammed the ship against our boat. Why were they so cruel and inhumane? Everyone on the boat screamed in fear; screams and cries were heard in the middle of the night on the pitch black sea. People shouted:

- Start the engine and run quickly.

- Why are you so cruel! Robbing money from peopleand not giving them chance to survive.

- You are devils!!

- The boat is broken, the water is in

The pirates laughed pompously amid the appalling cries of the boat people. Fortunately at that time, on the dark sea the boat was small and there were no lights, so they saw nothing, and left ...

ESCAPING

On the boat, young men tried to take turn bailing water, we all prayed to Buddha for salvation. As mentioned earlier, every time I prayed to Guan Yin, it was as if I saw her appear at the front of the boat, pulling the boat with her. Not knowing at that time whether I was awake or dreaming, or in the time of near death, my prayers as well as those of everyone came to an "ecstatic level", I could see Guan Yin appear to save sentient beings from sufferings.

It was true that thanks to Guan Yin guidance and protection, after the pirate ship left, the dilapidated boat still managed to float on the immense sea, along with Buddhist recitations all throughout the long night. Whenever we passed a fishing boat, though not seeing the people on it, but only the red light flashing in the distance, we did not dare to approach because of the lesson we learned from the recent misfortune. The boat manonly trusted the compass to move forward.

Everyone on board was tired. The two children,

exhausted from crying, fell asleep. I also fell asleep not knowing how long and woke up to hear a loud cry:

- Bird! We saw a bird!!!

Bewildered for a few seconds and looking out at the sea, I also saw from the distance a bird flying in the sky. There were many screams:

- Land, land!

- We survived!

Everyone was excited, the ship seemed revitalized. People sitting in the lower compartment heard the shouts, tried peeking through the hatch to catch a glimpse of the bird. The boat kept "charging" forward. I saw the blushing dawn on the far horizon, and felt more assured when darkness was over. After some time, we saw a flock of birds in the sky....

As expected, we were heading for the shore but we didn't know where it was. The boatman steered to keep the boat on the right for possible docking. But after a long distance we could not see a place suitable for landing, only the bottom with rocks of all sizes. The boatman told everyone that the boat could not go any closer, because there was too much water in the boat and the shore was too rocky.

He shouted:

- Please slowly get into the sea to wade in.

- Don't push each other to keep the boat from capsizing.

Everyone frantically jumped down. The young and people who could swim jumped down and waded to the shore amid the overexcited yelling and splashing water. A man shouted warning:

- Watch before jumping lest your head hit the reefs.

From the deck of the boat, through the clear water I could see rocks of all sizes below. Still struggling to know how to jump down because I could not swim and, seeing the rocks below, I thought it would not be too deep. Moreover because some people had jumped down, the boat lost balance, rocked from side to side as if about to be capsized. Holding my two children in my arms, I did not know how to bring them to the shore. I craned my neck to look for my two siblings and Nguyen, my nephew. Fortunately, I immediately met Thanh, a nephew of Mrs. Tu, owner of the house I stayed at the night in my-

aborted attempt to escape. As soon as he came up from the lower compartment, I pushed Tu to him and pleaded:

- Please take my son to the shore.

He was eager to help immediately, including helping to bring my nephew Nguyen. Then hurriedly picking up my youngest boy –with him held on my hip with my right arm and the bag on myleft shoulder – I jumped into the water. But... alas! The water level was far deeper than I thought. It was over my head. I tried to wave my arm for help; I saw death flashing before my eyes. At that time, everyone was worried about their own life. Nobody cared about anyone.

And yet!!! Our hour had not come. Someone saw my frantic waving. That person was Hoang, Thanh's younger brother. He had just waded ashore, and turning back to look at the ship he saw my arm. So he rushed out to save me and my son. That was truly my return to life from death. If Hoang had not run to the rescue, we would have drowned. Looking back at this situation later, I must believe in fate. If Hoang had not turned around to look at the ship, he would not have seen that I was in distress.

Still lying on the shore breathing heavily, suddenly I saw a young man prostrate next to me to kiss the ground, thenhe danced with joy for having reached the land. As for me, having sat on my haunches so long, I could not stand up, unable to stretch my legs. With great effort, I sat up and held my two children on my lap, tears welling up in my eyes. I cried out of joy for having just escaped death, and I felt the hardship and fear oppressing me in the past few days washed away by the water. Now on the shore of a strange land, my children and I had suddenly become miserable people in exile. While waiting for the villagers to report to the Thai authority, all of us gathered in a circle, exhausted and drained like wilted leaves.

SONGKHLA

While we waited for government officials to arrive, the villagers offered us food and water. Seeing the boat lying idle by the rocky shore, they immediately understood that we were refugees from Vietnam. So despite language difference, looking at their sympathetic gaze and their welcoming expressions, we were truly grateful.

Just over an hour later, Thai government employees arrived. Fortunately, the boatman–knowing Cambodian –translated for people what their government needed. When names and personal details were taken, I learned that the boat had 124 people in it. Wow! Thank God the boat did not sink. God had truly blessed us and brought us safely to shore.

After taking the list, government officials gathered us on a truck without a roof and drove us to the Thai police office about 20 kilometers away. When the truck started rolling, without exchanging a word, we all turned to look at the boat for the last time. The boat that had spent three nights and four days with us and took us across the sea in search of freedom, now rested lonely on the rocky shore, among the murmuring waves lapping against its sides. Although I knew I had been free, I could not help but shed tears. The boat was only an inanimate object, but it still deeply touched me when I had to leave.

On the way to the police station, seeing the Thai villagers living on both sides of the road – also in row houses with a garden like in Vietnam – their country was peaceful. They lived a frugal life, but not in fear like the Vietnamese people now suffering under the brutal yoke of the Communists. If they had not invaded the South and imposed their rule on my homeland, the people would not have to risk their life on the open sea. From now on Vietnamese people would become orphans exiled from their ancestral land.

I thought deeply about my eldest child and my two-extended families. From now on I would have to live in a strange land and would never be able to meet them again. It was a self-contradiction that we were determined to escape but now, having reached a strange land, I felt lost and lonely. Would this feeling haunt me and other boat people for the rest of our life?

The truck stopped in front of the police station, at the entrance of the office there was a sign written in Thai language but the only word I could recognize was Songkhla. Excitedly, I said to my two younger siblings:

- This is Songkhla!

To be sure, I asked a person there in English, probably he didn't know English, but just hearing me say 'Songkhla' with my finger pointing to the ground, he nodded in understanding. We actually reached Songkhla as planned.

When leaving, everyone just wanted to get out of Vietnam to go anywhere as long as they could escape. But just because my husband had reached Songkhla, everyone in the boat wanted to go to Songkhla, the only place they knew. In addition, Mrs. Sau said going to Thailand is nearer than going to Malaysia or Indonesia.

Waiting outside for the police to prepare the file and take fingerprint, everyone was tired after sleepless nights and especially the horrors of the journey. Some lay on the grass, some dozed off sitting with their bended knees, others huddled together to talk and chat. I saw my second son standing by an ice cream cart. I knew he wanted ice cream, but I didn't have a single cent with me. A Thai man and his son were on the way home from school, hisson – probably a few years older than my son – stopped at the ice cream cart and asked the father to buy it for him.

With a craving look, my child watched the boy eagerly savor the ice cream. My heart ached at the sight; after all, he was only a child, not knowing how to hide the hunger pang tormenting him. I ran over, trying to lead him away, but he resisted. I took him away but he kept looking back. Looking at us and the group of strange, haggard looking people in tattered clothes, the Thai man said something to the ice cream vendor, probably inquiring about us.

Then he immediately bought an ice cream and made sign to my son to take it. This scene had left a lasting vivid impression in my mind. Probably that was the most delicious ice cream my child had ever eaten in his life. I smiled and bowed my head to thank this kind Thai man.

When writing these lines, I asked my son if he still remembered that ice cream, and he said "How can I forget it". I was very surprised. The scene must have left a strong impact in his mind; he was just a 4-year-old at the time.

REFUGEE CAMP

After the formalities and finger printing, the Thai police drove us back in the direction of the sea. Everyone was afraid because while waiting at the police station I heard people exchanging rumor that some previous groups had been sent back to the sea. Our boatman asked the police escort where we were going, but they remained silent. Upon arrival, we were taken one by one into the police office. Here I also saw the sign in Thai characters also with the word Songkhla. But this office was smaller than the other place, and only a few policemen.

People got off the truck. On my right, there were rows of low houses with corrugated iron roofs, and tents teetering in the bright sunlight, barbed wire separating the two sections on either side of the narrow gate. Seeing the truck turn in and stop in front of the police office, a large number of people came running from the other side of the fence. Most men were shirtless, standing idly on the other side of the barbed wire fence. Everyone wore a towel or their shirt over their head to protect them from the scorching sun. They waved and called out to us.

I could not tellwhere they were from. If they were Thais, why were they locked up behind the barbed wire? If they were Vietnamese refugees, why they didn't look like us. They looked more like dark-skinned people in Africa. A few came out from the fence, waving and saying in Vietnamese that we had been accepted into Songlka refugee camp. Later I learned that they too were refugees who came before and were now working as camp security workers. They went out to help Thai police admit new people to the camp.

At this point everyone was assured not to be chased out to the sea, and had been admitted to the camp to be settledin a third country. Everyone was happy, so the new and old gathered together to ask about each other. We were discreetly advised by 'fellow camp residents' to hide valuable possessions such as money and gold before going through inspection by the police.

COINCIDENCE

While standing in line to enter the inner room to be searched by the police, I saw a young man struggling in the arms of a few persons, as if he tried to get out of the grip of these people. When getting close to the group they released him and pointed at me:

- Your wife and children, do you believe now?

This young man looked at me in bewilderment, I looked at him, and it took several seconds before we recognized each other. He turned out to be my husband! He did not recognize me; after only a few days at sea I no longer had my usual appearance. Also he did not expect me to dare taking the children across the sea. Myself, I also noticed that he had changed a lot; he was thinner, especially his complexion darkened from head to toes, he looked quite different from when he was at home. Just recognizing him, I burst into tears:

- Honey ! He... V... ũ...

Overwhelmed with emotion I was speechless. Alarmed, he turned sharply to me. Duyen hurriedly said:

- Vu has to stay behind.

Hugging the three of us he said with emotion:

- OK! OK! Please calm down. We'll talk about that later.

Turning to hug the two children, he continued:

- You are here and I am very happy. At first, seeing only the two of you my heart sank. Now knowing he couldn't go I feel assured. I thought he had gone but…

He didn't finish the sentence but I knew what he meant. If you had taken him with you against the advice of the family, we were not sure if he could survive the many dangers wehad gone through.

I asked him how he knew I was outside the gate. He said that a person working with the camp representative board was Phat. When the Thai police asked them to go out of the camp to help, Phat had seen me on the first trip and knew we were husband and wife. I only heardof Phat butdid not know his appearance. On the second trip, Phat went with my husband. In the camp, Phat noticed that my husband was always sad because the family was left behind. Phat had comforted him that maybe I would go on the next trip. But my husband told Phat that I and the children would definitely not go because he knew I was very cautious, and he himself had specifically said in the telegram home not to take the children with me. Life is full of surprise. Reality often turned out not as expected.

He continued:

- I was lying sadly in the tent when Phat and his friends rushed in to tell him that I and the children were at the gate doing paperwork for admission into the camp. I didn't believe them, thinking that, seeing I was so lonely and sad, they just wanted to tease me. Finally they grabbed me and carried me out here.

Because I also worked in the camp's representative board (publishing the camp bulletin), I was allowed to get out of the camp when new boat people arrived.

Taking advantage of the moment he was talking with us, a few people in my group – who had managed tokeep some gold –discreetly slipped their gold into his pants pockets to avoid being taken by the police.The gold would be returned to them after they had got inthe camp. That day, March 1, 1979, after being admitted into the camp,each family (people in the same list) was provided with necessary items such as blankets, food and old clothes, etc.People in the camp, who had been standing behind the barbed wire fence since this morning, had rushed out to greet us, calling out for each other, laughing and speaking loudly in the camp ground. It turned out that they had been standing there for hours waiting to see if there were relatives or friends among the newcomers. Some, meeting their acquaintances, impatiently asked for news from home, others, seeing no one were deeply disappointed...

In the new group, we were the only ones meeting

relatives in the camp. In the blink of an eye, news of our reunion had been known by everyone in the camp. Right at that time, there were delegations coming from Bangkok to interview asylum seekers for the third country. Reporters for CBS news learning about our case asked for an interview about our journey to be reunited with the family. I said to them:

- When I left, I did not know if I would reach Songkhla;on the immense sea how could I know where I was going. If lucky we survived otherwise we would be lost forever. Destiny had led my children and me to Songkhlato be reunited with my husband. Oh! I can't believe it, even in my dream. I think God blessed me.

LIFE IN CAMP

Because my husband had been here, I did not have to go through the trouble find people to sharethe shelter or to set up the tent myself. Songkhla refugee camp was right on the coast, since the day there were boat people coming by sea. The camp was not far from where my boat came ashore.

The living space was divided in two areas called 'lot'. One "lot", close to the office, was assigned to people who volunteered to work in the camp committee in charge of necessary activities such as security, news bulletin and entertainment, mail service, foods, health care,... Because of their volunteer work, they lived in a long one-story house with corrugated iron roof. Inside, there was only one wooden plank running from one end of the house to another with an entrance at every 10 meters.

Living space for sleeping only was assigned to people in the same list. (Cooking was done outside) So members of different families slept close to each other like sardines in a tin. Privacy was possible only at night when sleeping under a mosquito net.

At first, not used to living like that, I didn't feel comfortable. But then we got used to it. Everybody knew this place was just a temporary stop. Still it was better than being in the "tent", set up by the camp dwellers themselves. Although camp volunteers helped with making wooden pallet for the tent, the campers had to buy leaves, canvas or nylon sheets for the tent.

Whenever it rained, living conditions were even more difficult: rainwater poured into the tent, everything was blown away when heavy rain came with strong wind.

However, the advantage was that in front of each tent, a small makeshift bathing enclosure was set up for family use, so it was very comfortable. People living in the long house, on the other hand, had to use a common bathroom. Fortunately, my husband knew some people living in the tent, so we could take a bath with some privacy.

I started to get used to my new life at the refugee camp. The camp had about two thousand people by the time I entered the camp. Every morning when the sun came out, everyone heard the sermon of Father Bach over the loudspeakers. The campers were so familiar with his daily sermon that no one paid attention to his teachings anymore. They often stood in front of gate 1, waiting to go out to buy vegetables, meat and other miscellaneous items brought by the Thais. Although the Office of the United Nations High Commissioner for Refugees provided food for the campers, eating fish and the canned food every day could be tiring.

Those who received money from relatives abroad or had it with them when leaving did not need food from the High Commissioner. The buying and selling lasted only about three hours. So everyone wanted to be the first to go outside to buy what they needed, or exchanged money from US dollars to Thai currency.

At the camp, there were two distinct classes. Those having relatives abroad lived like a king. They ate fresh food, bought whatever they needed. They frequented the cafes in the camp; those who were alcoholics drank almost every day. Ear-splitting loud music constantly coming out of their tent.

The other class had no relatives, no extra support, lived quietly waiting for the day to go. These people were jokingly called "children of Catholic sisters". When gate 1 of the camp was closed after the shopping hours, it was time for people to fill the office area waiting for announcement of people having mail.

Boat people living in Songkhla camp could never forget the main road in the camp. This road was the dividing line between the living area on the left and the sea on the right. To meet friends or find acquaintances, you simply went along this main road. If you tookthe trouble of looking for them in their tent or in the long house you rarely found them. The reason was easy to understand: the house and tents were hot and cramped. People needed to go outside for the sea breeze and only returned at sleeping time. Moreover there was nothing to do in the camp, a lot of free time, beside learning English, people often went to the beach for fresh air, meeting friends chatting or bathing.

Later, after more than twenty years of sweat and toil working for a living in this second homeland of mine, my boat companions and I realized the time in the camp was the most enjoyable days. It was no different from the time we stayed at a holiday resort. At that time, surely every one of us had nothing to do but sitting by the sea, looking into a distant hazy future.

In the camp, going to the toilet was a rather complicated challenge. Even two rows of toilets could not accommodate the morning rush. Long line of people waited with a bucket of water in their hand to flush the toilet after use. Some smarty-pants pretended having urgent need to be given priority. But then the trick was discovered, and the 'courtesy for urgency' etiquette was no longer observed.

One thing made me laugh when I overheard the conversation of the two campers. While waiting in line to let my child go to the toilet, I heard two people asking each other:

- Why do you visit Uncle's mausoleum so late today?

- Oh! I had to go to the market early in the morning...

I wondered which uncle had a "mausoleum" here. I asked the people next to me and learned that the boat people in the camp called the toilet 'Uncle's Mausoleum'. I suddenly understood. It was only because of Uncle that the boat people had to risk their lives to be here. Oh! Whoever came up with this expression had really reached the pinnacle of "humor".

After a few days in the camp, my children and I were called to the office to be included into my husband's file. My two siblings and the nephew, being minors were also put in the same form. My husband, though having the sponsorship of his relatives in West Germany, had been approved by the US delegation and was on the waiting list of departure.

Every month, delegations of free countries around the world came to the camp to interview and selected boat people to their home countries. Some were lucky to be approved right away. Those not approved had to file an application to go to another country, or to ask for an appeal.

The United States was a country with the highest number of applications because most of them had relatives settled in US since the evacuation on April 30. Some of the people in the camp were former military personnel of the Republic, some were the civilians who had worked for American companies, and others wereadmitted on humanitarian ground. Since I had been included in my husband's application to go the US I waited for my departure date.

About a week after I stayed in the camp, one day the loudspeaker called my husband to the office to meet someone. It was the Lieutenant Colonel, commander of the Thai police station visiting him because he received word that his wife and children had been reunited with him at the camp. How my husband knew Lieutenant Colonel I would tell you later. All I knew and believed was that without dependent origination (nhân duyên), there will be no association or any relationship.

Thanks to him, my husband had been allowed to go downtown to send a telegram to let our parents know that the children and I had succeeded and we had been reunited. Without his help, my husband would have to write to his relatives in Germany and asked them to send a telegram to my parents who were anxiously waiting to hear from us.

About two months after my successful escape, one morning I received word that another sister had also escaped and was on an island called Kuku. This was the third success in our family, since the successful trip of my husband.

Because Kuku Island was a deserted island, it was said that Thai police would bring these people to Songkhla camp. I was happy for her successful escape but also felt pity for her having gone on the trip by herself at such a young age.

I went to the main gate every morning to see if anyone had been admitted to the camp. I waited like that the whole week before my sister and some other boat people were brought to the camp. Needless to say, we were so happy. It seemed that at that time, we were the only family reunited at the refugee camp. Although her boat didn't land at Songkhla, it was a blessing to be together at last.

DESERTED ISLAND

The next few nights my sisters and I lay on the sleeping platform to hear my youngest sister talking about life in the family after I left. Her story reminded us of the wonderful time living with our parents. Now we were living a wistful life in a refugee camp. She told me that after I left, my parents anxiously looked forward to hear about us every hour, every day. Although we were a big family, my mother missed me very much, probably she vaguely had a feeling that she might not see me again whether my trip was a success or a failure. Sometimes when going upstairs to take a nap, my mother wouldlisten to the cassette having my voice recorded from my unmarried days to feel as if I were still at home... Listening to my sister, I could'nt hold back my tears because, just like my Mom thought, we might not have a chance to see Mom and Dad again.

Back to the story after the day I left, there was no report of arrest, and instead Mrs. Sau's sent a message that the boat had left. Of course Mrs. Sau must be the first to know because members of her family were on that trip. But it was not known whether the boat had reached Songkhla. The whole family was extremely happy when receiving my telegram. During that time, Mom and my older sister went to visit and bring food to my brother, an officer kept in re-education camp. When she whispered into his ear the good news from us, he chuckled with a smile of hope, though he did not know when he would get out to see the clear sky of freedom.

In fact, after my successful escape, the whole family felt more reassured and had more confidence in the Mr. Sau and his wife. My elder sister asked my younger sister (who had just escaped) if she wanted to go again. But because I was arrested and jailed last time, she was scared. Moreover, she herself saw my mother being sad and miserable, longing for her child (after I left) so she did not want to hurt her mother any more. But with the depressing state of the country at that time, how could she hope for a bright future?

My sister's account

My trip was lost on a deserted island and we had to stay there for a week. This island was said to be "a godforsaken deserted island". When my ship beached there was no one single shadow insight besides the wreck of an 'semiofficial' refugee ship. We were told that the people in that boat had rushed to the mountain to hide from the pirates for fear of being robbed and raped. So I followed other people to go into hiding. On the way up the mountain, I saw skulls rolling in some places, and sometimes there were shrines for the unjust dead. Everyone was scared, everyone prayed for rescue by any fishing boat passing by.

If not killed by pirates, people would die of starvation and thirst. For a week we stood along the coast every day praying for any boat passing by. By the afternoon everyone had to climb the mountain to find a way to hide from the pirates. On the way back from fishing they would rush to the island to loot and rape. The situation was downright perilous and frightening. The mountain cliff had no place for a hand grip or a foothold. Together everybody had to hang on a rope in order not to get lost. Every day by 4.00 pm, when the sun was still shining, people had to get ready climbing up the mountain, before it got too dark to find the way, except when there was moonlight. The situation lasted for up to a week before we were rescued by a patrol ship of the Thai Navy.

Although people on my trip was tricked by pirates into a deserted island to be plundered and to live days of starvation and fear in the deserted island, it was lucky that no one was raped. Perhaps because at that time the refugee sea escape was still too new for the pirates, they only thought of robbing the goldrings and money of the boat people. Sometime later, when the sea escape became very common, the pirates not only tried to rob the boat people but they also raped women, including killing those who resisted.

End Of Sister's Account

A typical story I learned during my temporary stay at the camp was as follows. A boat was robbed by the pirates. They kidnapped four young girls and took them to their ship to rape them. They later sold them to brothels to force these girls to sell sex. Sometime later the girls escaped and ran to the police station to report and were then taken to Songkhla refugee camp.

They told the representative committee that a man trying to stop pirates raping his wife was killed with a hammer and thrown into the sea. The girls didn't know what happened to the boat afterward. Everyboat people voyage was filled with unforeseen dangers, in addition to hunger and thirst. Only the luckiest could hope to be spared of these perils.

Writing these lines I thought of a scene all the people and I at Songkhla camp witnessed around June or July of 1979. That afternoon people sitting by the sea saw from far away a boat coming toward the camp. At first they thought it was a fishing boat of local people. However, as the boat came closer, everyone realized it was a refugee boat with a lot of people standing on the deck. At the stern of the boat was a bamboo pole with a white shirt flapping in the wind. People in the camp shouted in unison:

- Refugee boat! Refugee boat! ...

People rushed to the shore. Immediately the loudspeaker in the camp announced the arrival of a boat. Someone ran out with a camera, took pictures of the boat approaching the shore (picture attached).

Not waiting for the boat to come to the shore, young people on the boat swam in to notify that there were people seriously injured, requiring urgent medical care.

When the victim was taken off the boat, alas, everyone saw that it was a girl only about 14 years old, covered in blood, her legs dangling as if about to fall off her body. Two young men carried the girl; another ran after her to keep her legs from dangling, blood dripping on the sand. They asked the Thai police for an ambulance.

People on this boat told us that they had been attacked by pirates. While climbing down from the pirate ship to her boat (just like the case of my boat) this girl was wounded and her legs were broken. People were not sure whether it was caused by the pirates ramming the boat or the boat was violently tossed against the pirate ship by strong waves.

Later we learned that one of her legs had to be amputated. Poor little girl, disabled at such young age. Only my boat and this boat reached Songkhla. The only difference was that this boat pulled right into the camp, and my boat was about 20 minutes' drive from the camp. But we were luckier, no one was injured or raped by the pirates.

Compared to the migration from the native land in the North of my parents and their generation in 1954, the refugee exodus from South Vietnam after 1975 was much more tragic and dramatic. People abandoned their home empty-handed, with nothing but shabby clothes on them, heading into an uncertain future in a strange land. On their perilous journey they ran the risk of drowning, life threatening injury and pirate attacks that robbed them not only their belongings but also destroyed their dignity. However, against this gloomy and dramatic panorama of history there were still a few heart-warming scenes of the benevolence and kindness of the Thai people which I would mention later.

Every evening after dinner, my husband and some

friends in charge of the newspaper section read news to the people in the camp, so that they knew what was happening in the world and their homeland, and received-information about life in the camp. After the news, they often re-broadcast the golden music heard on Saigon radio before 1975.

I remembered most the first night I entered the camp. After the news and story reading, we heard the recorded song "Darling! If our love had not been interrupted" by singer Nhat Thien Lan. Late at night, the passionate and sad lyrics of the song made many people in the camp, including those who were together, or had just been reunited like me broke into tears. It was even more poignant and heartbreaking for people who had gone away alone leaving their spouses and relatives behind.

On the other hand, at the camp with the gathering of so many people from different walks of life there happened quite a few personal tragi-comedies. Most boat people did not have personal papers. At the camp, they would list themselves as singles to be included in the same list with the person they had just met in the camp. All of a sudden, their spouse remaining in Vietnam was suddenly mercilessly abandoned. Or there are young people asking to be listed as newly married couple hoping they could leave the camp sooner. But when the marriage of convenience turned sour, they took each other to the office demanding to be separated. These incidents also caused a lot of headaches to the staff of the High Commissioner's Office.

If that was all then it would be simple. In addition to the above, every time a foreign delegation came to interview the refugees, volunteers in the group helped people to fill out forms, interpreted or wrote appeal forms in English. My husband had the opportunity to witness many respectable heroes. A former officer of the ARVN Airborne troops, after answering fluently many questions from the American delegation, thought it was finished. But the head of the delegation added another question as if he had not believed the statement of the ARVN officer.

- What kind of gun did you use? M16, colt, submachine, machine gun?

- As a commander I have to know everything.

- So how many bullets M16 has? How many bullet machine gun has?

Instead of answering the question, the former soldier could not contain his anger; he snatched the application from the hands of the American interviewer and declared:

- I don't need to go to America!!!

Then he got up and walked out of the room to the astonishment of the American delegation, the interpreter and other people present. That soldier had good reason for his behavior. The head of the American delegation was a person having power but no dignity. While interviewing the refugees, he only wore a short, showing his hairy bare chest as if he was about to go for a swim.

Granted that the weather in Asian countries was always hot, but at least he had to dress to suit his position. In the interviews he was always rude, arrogant, showing contempt for boat people and acting as if he had the power of life and death over the interviewee. Everyone in the camp knew that. But most people chose to close their eyes and "hold their breath while crossing the bridge" so that they could soon settle down where they wanted to go. But there was still a number of people like the airborne soldier who, out of a sense of nationalistic pride, felt that the haughty behavior of the head of the US delegation must be checked.

One day when my husband was helping people to get ready for the interview. Two persons, father and son, came out with a worried face. Meeting my husband, the father lamented:

- Maybe I was refused to go to the United States! If so please help me write an appeal.

- Why do you think so? What did the American delegation say?

- Because when I came in for the interview, seeing a chair in front of the American chief, I sat down to answer questions like the one who came before me. But the man banged on the table saying why I dared to sit down before receiving his permission.

Hearing this, my husband was annoyed with the behavior of the head of the American delegation. Only yesterday another man came for the interview. Although he saw the chair in front of him, he did not dare sit down, he meekly stood still in a daze with a frightened look, and the head of the American delegation shouted:

- The chair is there why you don't sit down.

The interviewee hurriedly sat down. This incident, of course, was passed on to the otherpeople so that they could avoid making the mistake. Ironically, this man and his son had been scolded and son when they sat down.

My husband felt that the Vietnamese needed to show their attitude to let this American know that we lost South Vietnam, but we did not lose our self-respect and honor. Discontent about those incidents, and witnessing the rude, andcontemptuous behaviorof the leader of the American delegation – that he called the "butcher" –my husband decided not to apply to go to the United States anymore. Later, having settled in a third country, I didn't know whether his decision had been due to his wisdom, or to our destiny.

SETTLEMENT AND DESTINATION

After deciding to cancel our plan to settle in the US, my husband had listened to the persuasion of his relatives who had gone to study and settle in West Germany since the Second Republic (1967-1975). This man had sent a letter of sponsorship to my husband since his arrival at the camp, as I mentioned previously. He said life in Germany was very gratifying. The refugees were taken care of very well by the government. In fact, unaccompanied teenagers – dubbed 'children of Catholic sisters'–, people with disability were all received and treated very nicely by West Germany. They sent letter to the camp telling their friends so.

Those who settled in America wrote that they were not supported as well as in Germany, except those who have relatives. I had not lived in any country, and only learned from the letters sent to their family from those who had gone. But seeing the conduct of the American delegation, everyone understood. On the other hand delegations from other countries, such as Germany, France, Australia, and Canada, were considerate; they interviewed boat people with a warm and relaxed attitude without being condescending. So we both agreed to settle in West Germany.

My settlement story was equally remarkable as my journey at sea. One day I went to the representative office to look for my husband. At that time, the Canadian and French delegations came to interview and do paper works.While waiting,I sat on an empty chair nearby. After a while I saw a lady walking towards me, looking around, and smiling at me. I suddenly understood and was about to get up, asking her:

- This seat is yours, isn't it?

She smiled and nodded but signaled me to sit down. But I still got up to return her seat:

- Sorry I do not know.

- Do you work up here?

- No. My husband does.I come to look for him.

Noticing me speak a little English, she spoke to me, asked me what my name was, how long I was the camp, and whether I had been accepted by any country. She introduced herself as apastor's wife. The couple came with a Canadian delegation to the refugee camp to evangelize. I told her that I could have gone to America, but later changed to West Germany. She asked me why I didn't want to go to Canada. Her country is a democratic and free country. Life of the people was well taken care of by the government, especially health care. At that time, I did not know about that. Among the people at the camp who had settled before me, no one said anything about life in Canada. We only knew it was cold all year round. However, I nodded in acknowledgement and smiled hesitantly:

- But Canada is so cold.

She reassured me:

- Yes, it's cold, but you will get used to it. Winter lasts only 3 months. In my country there are four seasons, every season has its beauty.

Then she avidly told a few stories about the four seasons in her country, which I could not understand very much. I thought:

- My English was not so good, but you kept talking so well...

To conclude the story, she asked me:

- So do you want to go to Canada? Let me tell the people in the delegation to give you an application.

Before I could answer, she turned to a white man sitting at the table with many files and handed me an application. I didn't want to disappoint her for the conversation we just had. Moreover the lady was kind and sympathetic, so I accepted the application from her just to please her. She even asked me if I had time to sit down to write the application. But I told her I had to go. Before taking leave, she told me that she would only stay here for one more day and that I'd better submit the application as soon as it was completed.

On the way back to our living quarter, I was about to throw the application away, thinking that we had finished the paperwork to go to West Germany, and I didn't know if my husband would change his mind. Also changing the country of settlement would take more time. Nevertheless, I still told my husband about my conversation with that lady.

After listening to me, my husband still wanted to go to West Germany and did not want to change the plan, (as I had expected) so I did not fill out the application. I thought of the kindness and concern of this lady in this casual meeting that afternoon. Although my husband did not want to fill out the application, I completed it anyway. So the head of household in the application was my name.

The next day I brought in the application only to meet her and let her know I appreciated her kindness and had listened to her "preaching" about a good Canada. But in the application, I deliberately did not attach photos of my family so that the application would be incomplete and therefore not considered. Yet before leaving the camp, people in the delegation called me to say that photos were required for the application. I offhandedly replied that I didn't have the money to have the pictures taken, I would submit them later. I said that just for the sake of courtesy, but I knew my application would be thrown into the trash bin. Moreover, we had decided to go to West Germany, so certainly the Canadian delegation or any other delegation would not accept us anymore. I applied just to show my appreciation of her kindness and she wouldn't feel disappointed because the application would be reviewed by the head of the Canadian delegation, not the pastor's wife.

But a month later, my name was on the list of the Canadian delegation sent to the camp; these people could go to Bangkok to have a medical examination within a week. Hearing my name over the loudspeaker, we were surprised. My husband rushed to the representative board to find out if it was true. I thought that without the photos, the application would not be approved, yet it was. Now that Canada's approval came before Germany's we were caught in a dilemma. All our luggages had been labeled with the destination address in Germany and we just waited for the list from the German delegation.

The rule of the camp was that when a person was on the list of a delegation, that person must leave the camp as scheduled. So my husband had to come to the High Commissioner's office to appeal. He also contacted the Thai Police Lieutenant Colonel who came to visit us to ask him for a way to help us stay in the camp for the list of the German delegation.

At the turn of this event, my husband's friends at the camp about to go to America or Canada, advised him to follow what had happened: take whatever come first. It would be more convenient to visit each other because all would settle in North America. Out of deference to our friends and, myself, I believed whatever happened, either bad or good, was all due to fate. Not everything we wanted to would come true, and the unexpected might actually happen. So I told my husband not to appeal but just accepted to go to Canada. With that decision, we changed the destination address on our luggages.

Once again we had to give up another country that initially we thought we would accept to resettle. The decision not to choose West Germany made my husband-feel apologetic towards a Vietnamese family. This family was very close to my husband; the head of the family used ask my husband for help with the paperwork and translation. He used to be an owner of a tailor shop in Saigon. In the camp, he made a living by making clothes for those about to leave for in a third country, so his life at the camp was very prosperous. His family was approved to go to the United States, for humanitarian reason. Seeing my family abandon the USfor West Germany, he also did the same, partly because of his fondness for my husband. Who could have thought that in the end, our settlement would be changed? So his family had to go to West Germany alone without us as companions.

We left the camp before him, so we didn't know what his family's life would be like. From then on every time I talked about our life in the camp, my husband still felt guilty about that. Undoubtedly, in our worldly life, reunion and separation was always ordained by predetermined factors. How else could our settlement be arranged without the hand of fate? Maybe many people didn't believe in destiny. But my life story must have convinced these people otherwise.

A week after the list of the Canadian delegation was sent to the camp, we completed the formalities to be transferred to the transit camp. The day I left camp also made me feel dispirited. Although I did not want to stay in this shelter much longer, but in the previous months, this place had supported our family in particular and the entire boat people in general. How could we not feel any emotional attachment when leavingit. The day before we left the camp, we transferred all the clothings, blankets, including pots and pans, dishes, etc., in general, all the necessities to those who stayed behind.

    The night before we left, friends in the camp invited us to a farewell tea party. This "tradition" had been around since the establishment of the refugee camp, I was told. Not sure who was the first to invent this parting tea party. I thought it was probably because of the limited resources of life in the camp, friends and neighbors – who had lived together in the days of wandering without material and spiritual comfort – wanted to share a homely sweet bowl of custard as an expression of feelings for each other to send their friends to a new promised land. So it became a custom that every time someone left the camp, the last night was always a time to have tea with friends and neighbors. In the morning before boarding the bus, we also had a souvenir photo taken with friends who still remained to celebrate and mark the beginning of a new journey.

TRANSIT CAMP

From Songkhla camp to Bangkok it took more than a day's journey. Sitting on the bus with my husband, my siblings and children, I thought of the time when my children and I took the bus to go down to the sea with the anxiety, bewilderment and fear of being arrested. Today also on the bus, although the seats are comfortable, and the passengers were not afraid of the sound of whistle to stop the bus for checking personal ID,for harassment or arrest, my heart still felt heavy. Was it because every move was a further distance away from my homeland. This trip would probably be a farewell forever.

I remembered the conversations between my mother and her clients in the past. They complained to my mother that because of the difficult life, they had to leave their native Central region to settle in Saigon to earn a living. In such narrative I felt their suffering having to leave their native land. But from the Central to the South of my country it was not so far, because it was still my home country, still in our motherland. Compared to the case of my family and that of other boat peoplefleeing the country in search of freedom and democracy, and seeking asylum in a foreign country, this was really a heartrending feelingof loss for our homeland.

Arriving at the transit camp in Bangkok, everyone must have a medical examination before leaving for the third country. As for my family, the first job was to have our photos taken, and then the health examination because, as I mentioned above, my application was submitted without photos.

Transit camp is a four-storey hotel.The guests did not have to cook; meals were provided by the hotel. So every morning, after waking up,those having money could take care of their own breakfast, otherwise, around 10 a.m. guests would start standing in line to receive lunch. Altogether there were about a few hundred people so if you wanted to eat lunch at lunch time you had to start queuing up around 10 a.m. to receive your meal around noon otherwise you wouldn't get your lunch until after noon. The Thais in charge of cooking had to start cooking from 8am. because they had to cook many times.

As soon as lunch was over, they had to prepare dinner. And around 4 p.m. the guests had started standing in line. Some people lined up early, got their food early and later if, still feeling hungry, they returned to stand in line again for a second serving. There was no restriction. If you were hungry, just stood in the line to be served.

Therefore, at the transit camp, there were only two things to do: standing in line for daily food and drink, and going to the clinic for medical examination. Depending on the health of each person, the result might take a long or short time. Some people with weak lungs or spots were called back and forth for re-examination. They had to spend all day waiting at the clinic.

During this period of more than a month in this transit camp, I would never forget the sleepless nights watching my youngest son who was constantly sick. Every time he had a high fever he had seizures and convulsions, his eyes turned white. I was very scared; there were nights when my husband and I had to take turn to sit and watch him, lest in his seizure he would bite his tongue. Once in my panic I hurriedly put my finger into his mouth and got bitten by him. Although my body hurt, my mind was at peace because at least I could keep the safety of my child's life.

MY HUSBAND'S ACCOUNT OF HIS TRIP

As I mentioned above, my husband's second attempt was also extremely adventurous, I would like to tell you briefly to give you some facts about how my husband met Lieutenant Colonel, Provincial Police Chief N.Following is his account:

January 4, 1979:departed from Saigon to Rach Gia

January 5, 1979:took small boat to big boat.

January 6, 1979:no rendezvous with big boat, returned to the mainland, hid in the forest.

That morning, it was still dark and we were taken to the big boat. Everything went well but no big boat at rendezvous point. People on small boats anxiously waiting.After about an hour still nothing happened. Boatmen on the small boats afraid of being arrested had to disperse. They did not dare to bring people back to the starting point for fear of being discovered. They only took people a short distance and asked everyone on the boat to jump into the river and wade ashore. It was still pitch dark at the time;one could not see one's own hand in the dark, let alone finding the way back. When coming to Rach Gia, I had a guide, and now everyone told me to find my way on my own. But still, I was forced to leave the small boat.

Water level was up to everybody's neck and the river bottom was very muddy, yet everybody kept running to save himself. I was completely disoriented, I only moved in the direction of dim electric lights in the distance. I prayed to Guan Yin to show me the way to Rach-Gia market. Coming close to some houses, I was terrified by the loud barking of dogs for fear of being discovered and arrested. The whole night, with the bag on my head to keep the clothing dry, I kept on wading and fervently praying for my survival.

Miraculously, as if guided by an invisible hand, I found the way to the main road where there were three-wheeled Lambrettas and trishaws passing by. I stood by the road to wait for a vehicle, whistling a [popular revolutionary] tune "As if Uncle Ho ..." – pretending to be a homebound 'vanguard youth' to avoid the attention of local people. Without such a cover-up, I would be easily suspected by the police and militia with my whole body wet and muddy, and my appearance of not being a local person. I hailed three-wheeled Lambretta already packed with people, but for some reason the driver stopped to pick me up. He pointed with his chin at a space next to him, implying that it was the only space available. Then he asked in a whisper:

- Get away?

Not sure why I did not try to lie to the driver at the time. I looked at the driver, nodded slightly and whispered:

- I have no more money. Please give me a ride back to Rach Gia.

Perhaps surprised at my honesty, or also sharing the hatred of a people deprived of freedom, the driver wanted to help the escapee and whispered to me:

- Sit still, I'll take you there.

Before getting off the vehicle, I graciously held the driver's hand to show my gratitude that he did not report to the police, nor charged an exorbitant fare, but instead helped me get to where I wanted to go.

At Rach Gia market, I had absolutely no idea where I was going. I tried to recall the way I had taken with the guide to Phat's house the day before – where I had spent the previous day –but I absolutely couldn't remember. The market was very crowded and had many alleyways, andit was late in the evening. Even if one wanted to pay attention from the beginning, it would be impossible to remember the way.

Yet, from the time being in abandoned the middle of nowhere I always recited prayers to Guan Yin, begging for guidance to Phat's house to contact Mr. Sau and his wife. Finally, I made it to Phat's house, as if led blindfoldedby an invisible hand. If it weren't for the miracle, how could I find the house I wanted to go to?

Coming to a house, it suddenly dawned upon me that in front of the house there was a three-wheeled cart with a broken wheel leaning against a wooden platform. That was the only clueI still remembered of Phat's house. I knocked on the door and it was Phat who opened the door, his head newly shaved. Seeing me, Phat was surprised and asked how I got there. I said that I myself did not know, all I knew was that I just kept praying Guan Yin to show the way. Phat told me:

- I was lucky to escape. I made a vow to shave my head as a gesture of gratitude

It was normal for Phat to come home, because Phat was a local person. Fortunately, the police did not catch him when he was left off on the river. But my return to Phat's house was indeed a miracle. He himself could not believe that it happened.

January 8, 1979

After staying at Phat's house for two days, I was led to the boat by a person of Mrs. Sau's family. It was said that the other night the big boat did not dare to appear for fear of being discovered by the police. And now everyone came back for a second attempt.

I suddenly remembered the fortune teller saying to my mother before my husband's departure: "Inauspicious beginning, auspicious ending". Until now, my husband did not know if anyone had been arrested that night while trying to wade ashore.

My husband continued:

January 10, 1979

After two days on the sea my boat ran into the pirate ship. Like many other boats, my boat was also robbed – twice in one day – but fortunately no one was assaulted or raped. Both times robbed I managed to hide the wedding ring. This ring had escaped the search of the police when I was imprisoned. And on this second trip the pirates forced everyone to give them all the gold and money. Anyone discovered trying to hide it would be beaten. I held the ring in my mouth. Seeing the pirate making the other person open his mouth to be checked, I thought I couldn't get away. But when I gave my watch to the pirate, the latter didn't make me open my mouth anymore. It was a close call! Later, I realized that it was foolish to do so because if the pirate found it, I would surely be beaten up.

By the next day, my boat broke down, and the boatman had to use an outboard motor. Then the storm came, the ship seemed about to sink under the crashing waves. Water flooded the ship, the young men traveling alone like me had to bail the water out of the boat and helped with the boatman to steer the ship. Other men went with their families and children only took care of their family members while those busy bailing the water were hungry and had no rest. Many people were angry with this type of selfish people who cared nothing about others.

As soon as the boat reached international waters, they killed a chicken to hold a celebration meal for their own family. Perhaps they thought being relatives of the ship owner, they had the privilege to do so? Some people on the boat complained that they should not commit such an act of killing, especially in this perilous crossing when everyone must do many good deeds to deserve the protection of the Almighty. Unfortunately, some people do not have such knowledge.

January 11, 1979

Running with an outboard motor until the next morning, the boat stalled and drifted to a place that looked like a Thai fishing village, very close to the border of Malaysia. The boat stayed there for two days, and the villagers provided food and water. The people there were very poor. So poor that my jeans hung up at night to dry was nowhere to be seen in the morning.

On the third day, Thai police came to meet people on the boat. They gathered everyone and drove to the police station to meet the police chief. This was a Thai tourist resort, so while sitting in the yard waiting for the police interview people were offered food and water by the Thai tourists. In my life I had never had a can of Coca and a piece of sandwich so delicious.

After nearly a week, the Lieutenant Colonel Police chief of this province announced that he received order from his superior not to admit the boat people and everyone had to get back on the boat to go somewhere.

Everyone was so terrified and pleaded with him not to do so because the boat was too damaged to run. But he said it was an order from above, he had no choice but to comply; in his heart he really wanted to help but he had no power.

With an imploring look at the Lieutenant Colonel, I begged him for help. The boat was seriously damaged; it was a blessing that the group had landed here. The people on board were mostly women and children who were sick and hungry, desperately in need of a shelter. Now, if pushed back to the sea, they would surely lose their life. After a long silence he told me he would try to find a solution and let the people know.

HEART OF A BODHI

Lieutenant Colonel Thai Police Officer

While waiting, everyone – irrespective of their faith –fervently and wholeheartedly prayed to be allowed to stay in Thailand and not to be pushed to the sea again. But life was not simple; one must act according to the laws of the country and not simply according to the love of God or the compassion of Buddha. As a result, the boat still had to obey the laws of the higher authority; it had to be towed to the sea.

The policemen were ordered to repair the boat so that it could continue sailing. The hope of staying was dashed. But fortunately, the group met a man - the police chief with a heart of a Bodhi – who used his wisdom to carry out his superior's order and also save the people. Knowing that it was impossible to change the order of a higher authority the Lieutenant Colonel discreetly said to me:

- I was ordered to push you back to the sea tomorrow morning. But remember to tell your compatriots to stay calm on the boat, and all of them must gather as far as possible toward the bow of the boat.In the twilight, I will tell my soldiers to lead the boat out to sea.By an accident your boat would be 100% damaged,then I would have a reason to rescue it and let your people stay. But please keep this only between you and me, lest I would be implicated for not following order.

I was overwhelmed with emotion. Tears brimming in my eyes, I could not believe that in this world, a total stranger with no relationship to my people and my country could so wholeheartedly extend his help. It must be said that the police chief had saved my life and the life of people on the boat.

January 17, 1979

It was exactly as planned by the police chief. That morning I advised everyone to follow the police chief's order to get back to the boat because there was no other choice. Everyone cried out, some prostratedbefore the Lieutenant Colonel. Some people refused to get on the boat because they saw that was certain death. Only I knew that we would be saved. But since I had promised to keep it a secret, how could I tell the people. So I coaxed people to get on to the boat but told everyone to gather near the bow of the boat.

As the Lieutenant Colonel had said,the Thai Navy ship towed our boat out a distance. Then they turned around and somehow 'accidentally' hit the stern of the boat. People screamed in horror. Immediately the police chief sent soldiers out to the rescue. With the evidence that the ship was damaged, everyone was allowed to stay to complete the formalities for temporary residence in Thailand. Unaware of the Lieutenant Colonel's benevolence,people bore a grudge against him. A good deed from the heart needs no public recognition.

I myself went to see the police chief to express deep gratitude for what he had done to save the entire group. This gratitude for his kindness opened the way tomy friendship with the police chief during my stay. He helped me as if he were a close friend, taking me to send the telegram home, inviting me to his home to take shower and eat with his family during the temporary stay.

END OF MY HUSBAND'S ACCOUNT

January 26, 1979

After two weeks of waiting, people in the same boat with my husband were finally admitted to Songkhla refugee camp. When leaving the province, my husband though the would lose contact with the colonel. But on the contrary, sometimes he drove a jeep to the refugee camp to visit and bring supplies for my husband. When I was admitted to the camp, he also brought his wife to visit to share the joy. Even when we were transferred to the transit camp in Bangkok, he and his wife also dropped in and took us out to eating, sightseeing in the city of Bangkok– his main residence was in Bangkok.

After settling in the third country, we kept in touch with his family by correspondence. Sometimes later, when the children had grown up, we had time to travel and also visited his family a few times. Every time we met, they still gave us the feeling of being his family members and treated us with deep affection.

It was very touching that once we happened to visit him right on the occasion of the birthday of his wife, we were invited to attend the birthday ceremony. I was told that in Thai customs only family members and relatives could attend this ceremony. After years of police service in his homeland, he rose to the rank of Lieutenant General, and he is now a senator of Thailand.

Miss Kai

In the premise of the hotel in Bangkok, which served as a transit station for all boat people in Thailand, there was a stall selling groceries such as bread, butter, milk, pastries and dry goods kept by the daughter of the hotel manager and his wife. Her name was Kai, a student at Bangkok University. Every morning, before going to school she came to open the store for the shopkeeper.

I often brought my children here to buy milk or candy,so she and I became friends as if we were classmates. Kai loved my two children, especially the youngest. Whenever coming to the store, Kai would go to our room to hold the boy and give gifts. There were days Kai would stay with us for a long time. Kai asked about Vietnam, the capital of Saigon that I had left against my will. I told Kai about what I and other boat people had gone through on the sea. Tears came to her eyes when she learned about the price boat people had paid to reach the shore of freedom. As our friendship grew closerI learned that Kai family owned the hotel that the Office of the High Commissioner for Refugees had contracted to serve as transit accommodation for boat people.

Sometimes Kai brought us to the city to dine out and buy books to learn English. Once at a bookstore, my husband stood a long time eagerly reading an electronic magazine. Then he put it backto the shelf. At that timeit was a luxury to us, we had to save money just in case our children got sick. Yet the next day Kai bought that magazine and brought it to my husband.

On the day we left the camp, Kai took time from school to send us off. She put an envelope in my hand, inside was a very sentimental letter, and a picture of Kai as a souvenir. Before we boarded the bus, Kai hugged my two children a long time as if she did not want to leave them. I saw Kai wiping tears in her eyes as the bus started. On the plane, I wondered why among hundreds of people in that place, only my family and Kai had such a loving attachment. Was that because our relationship in our previous life had made us feel sad when we were separated in this life?

A few years later, we got news of Kai's marriage. From halfway around the world, we sent Kai our wedding gift. But I knew perhaps the spiritual gift that Kai cherished most was our mutual, dearest and lasting friendship.

On our turbulent journey, my husband and I were so fortunate to meet such beneficent people who had saved as well as helped us with loving heart. People like the Thai Lieutenant Colonel, Miss Kai, HL in prison, the Lambretta driver in RachGia, the former captain on the same boat with us, two young men Thanh and Hoang who saved us from drowning... Maybe empathy and affinity help bring people together.

Help comes from the heart. Not everyone is kind, there are selfish people who only think of themselves and turn a blind eye to others in difficulty.

With this thought, I remembered the day I came to the camp. A woman ran in to congratulate my husband and me. I learned from her the circumstance of her getting to know my husband. The first day she entered the camp she had no shelter and her youngest nine-year-old child was seriously ill. About to sleep, my husband heard somebody moaning, he looked out and saw this woman and her children lying on a nylon sheet on the ground and it was pouring rain at the time. She just cried,and my husband saw that her son was sick with high fever. He hurriedly got up and gave up the tent, blanket for the mother and her child. Deeply moved and grateful for such a gracious act she often visited us.

This story suddenly reminded me of the benefactor in jail with my husband who had given up the mosquito net and his place for my son. The blessings bestowed on my husband, he had passed them on to others. I think blessings, and favors are like flames of love that we ought to keep burning and pass on to others. Only by that way that we can help reduce sufferings in this world.

When the World Airways DC-9 jetliner departed

from Bangkok airport. I knew from that time Saigon only lived in my mind, as a nameless memory, a wound that never healed in the heart of every boat people.

In the third country people looked at me with "admiration". They said I was very brave to have taken two children across the sea by myself. I said that anyone in the situation of boat people like us would do the same. Freedom is the priceless.

Mộng Thường
April, 2014

Liên lạc Tác giả
Mộng Thường
thucle2015@gmail.com

Liên lạc Nhà xuất bản
Nhân Ảnh
han.le3359@gmail.com
(408) 722-5626

www.ingramcontent.com/pod-product-compliance
Lightning Source LLC
Chambersburg PA
CBHW030527080526
44586CB00011B/346